Philosophizing the Everyday

Revolutionary Praxis and the Fate of Cultural Theory

JOHN ROBERTS

Pluto Press

LONDON • ANN ARBOR, MI

First published 2006 by Pluto Press
345 Archway Road, London N6 5AA
and 839 Greene Street, Ann Arbor, MI 48106

www.plutobooks.com

Copyright © John Roberts 2006

The right of John Roberts to be identified as the author of this work has been
asserted by him in accordance with the Copyright, Designs and Patents Act
1988.

British Library Cataloguing in Publication Data
A catalogue record for this book is available from the British Library

ISBN 0 7453 2411 8 hardback
ISBN 0 7453 2410 X paperback

Library of Congress Cataloging in Publication Data applied for

10   9   8   7   6   5   4   3   2   1

Designed and produced for Pluto Press by
Chase Publishing Services Ltd, Fortescue, Sidmouth, EX10 9QG, England
Typeset from disk by Stanford DTP Services, Northampton, England
Printed and bound in the European Union by
Antony Rowe Ltd, Chippenham and Eastbourne, England

Contents

Preface

This book began its life as an essay for *Radical Philosophy*, 'Philosophizing the Everyday: the philosophy of praxis and the fate of cultural studies', published in 1999. Since then the arguments of my essay have gradually expanded their range, as the need to probe and develop my history of the concept of the everyday became a priority in the face of the increasingly ubiquitous (and vague) use of the concept in contemporary cultural studies and other disciplines. Moreover, I felt I needed to nuance and clarify my own use of the term from my previous work. In 1998 I published *The Art of Interruption: Realism, Photography and the Everyday*. The book looked at how photography in the twentieth century developed at the intersection of the philosophical claims of realism and the cultural claims of the 'everyday', and how this in turn transformed the concept of the everyday in cultural theory. However, my emphasis was primarily on a discussion of the relationship between photographic form and everyday 'modes of attention' – as subscribed to by the early Soviet and Weimar avant-gardes. I didn't actually discuss the critique of the everyday as *praxis*, the defence of which had an overwhelmingly, indeed hegemonic, influence on revolutionary theory and Marxist theories of cultural democracy and transformation during the first half of the twentieth century. *Philosophizing the Everyday* remedies this omission by reclaiming and reflecting on this extraordinary range of the literature of the everyday, in order to draw on its continuing philosophical and political vitality for cultural work today. In this I direct my focus of attention to the history of the concept itself.

I would like to thank Peter Osborne of *Radical Philosophy* for his initial interest in this project, and Esther Leslie whose own interest in the subject and guest editorship at Pluto along with Mike Wayne has seen this project come to fruition. Thanks also to Anne Beech and David Castle, and Michelle as always, for their support.

Prologue: Dangerous Memories

Recently the concept of the everyday has undergone a widespread revival. It is the subject – or reference point – of a wide range of books and essays on art, architecture, design, urban studies, anthropology and political science, as well as being the interdisciplinary theme of many recent art exhibitions and cultural events.[1] On these grounds the concept has become the common currency of much contemporary discourse on art and popular culture and cultural studies. After modernism, after postmodernism, it is argued, the 'everyday' is where art goes, not only to recover its customary and collective pleasures, but to display its own ordinariness, just as it is also the place where the pleasures of popular culture are indulged and negotiated, from soap operas to celebrity magazines and out-of-town shopping stores. The everyday is the place where we supposedly define and shape our common pleasures, a place where a democracy of taste is brought into being. In this way the current ease with which the term is identified with the popular, and the ease with which it is able to pass between disciplines and practices, suggests that the everyday has now become, above all else, a meta-signifier of social and cultural inclusivity. The everyday is demotic, spectacular, interactive – all things to all people, in fact – a space where the worlds of design, architecture, fashion and art coalesce, compete and constellate.[2] Indeed, use of the term is now something of an ecumenical fetish: evidence of the up-to-dateness of each discipline's interdisciplinarity.

Philosophizing the Everyday is a response to this contraction of the concept of the everyday into a theory of consumption

1

and simple cognate of 'ordinariness', an attempt, in short, to reinstate the philosophical and political partisanship of the concept. For, with the broad assimilation of the term into contemporary cultural studies, the 'everyday' has suffered from not only a general process of critical dehistoricization but an acute philosophical foreshortening. In an eagerness to borrow from what is most amenable to postmodern theories of the productive consumer, contemporary debates on the everyday have severed the concept's connections to prewar debates on social agency, the cultural form of art, and cultural democratization. Too much contemporary theory is eager to limit the critique of the everyday to a theory of signs and patterns of popular cultural consumption or the dilemmas or ambiguities of representation. This is not the place to analyse in any great detail how this conception of the everyday has shaped the recent history of cultural studies. But, suffice it to say, cultural studies' use of the everyday remains largely locked into a prevailing 'redemptive' model, in which the creative powers of the consumer operate freely in the heartlands of mass culture. Since the 1980s and the formative theorization of these moves in terms of working-class subcultural 'practices of resistance', cultural studies has tended to follow the direction of Michel de Certeau's work: creative consumption is to be identified with the popular memories and counter-knowledges and histories to be found in the workings of ideology (see Chapter 2). As one author on the everyday and cultural studies has argued recently, in de Certeauian terms, what remains significant about the everyday is how it escapes or defeats our rational attempts to locate and describe it.[3] The critical importance of the redemptive model of cultural studies is not in doubt in its exposing of the intellectual condescension towards 'non-professional' cultures or popular experience. But if a critical concept of ideology needs a conception of culture, then a critical concept of culture needs a conception of ideology.[4] In this, cultural studies' increasing focus on the autonomy of popular agency has weakened the grasp of ideology (and as such diminished the theory of alienation in the analysis and critique of the popular).

The de Certeauian model has emerged as a belated theory of the everyday in Anglo-American cultural studies, overstepping the works of Henri Lefebvre, whose important writing of the 1950s and 1960s on the everyday was only translated into English in the 1990s. As such there is no systematic Lefebvrian or Marxist engagement with the concept of the everyday in Anglo-American cultural studies before the rise of de Certeau's influence.[5] As late as 1993, for example, Stanley Aronowitz in a thorough survey of the rise and fall of Anglo-American cultural studies only mentions the everyday in passing and without any conceptual weight.[6] It is no surprise, therefore, why the 'everyday' is so politically and philosophically depleted in contemporary cultural studies: in its eagerness to critique an older cultural studies it bypasses the richness and complexity of the concept's early history.

This book does something different: it maps out the pre-Second World War debates on the everyday in order to reinstate the concept's complex and contested history as the basis for a *critique of culture*, beginning from the modern origins of the term in Freudian psychoanalysis and the Russian Revolution to the concept's critical reinvention (and more familiar extension) in postwar France. Indeed, the emergence of the concept of the everyday in the first three decades of the twentieth century is the outcome of four interrelated sets of far-reaching critical practices: (1) the Leninist extension of politics into cultural politics during and after the Russian Revolution (Trotsky's cultural activism; Soviet Productivism and Constructivism); (2) the transformation of European Marxism into a philosophy of praxis out of Marx's critique of traditional materialism and the return to Hegel and the philosophy of consciousness (Georg Lukács, Karl Korsch, Antonio Gramsci, Walter Benjamin, Lefebvre); (3) Freud's demedicalization of mental disorders and illness; and (4) the emergence of the new avant-garde documentary art and literature. At some points these overlapping practices repulse each other, at other points they interfuse, yet what they produce overall is an extraordinary attentiveness to the political form and significance of cultural activity and change. Revolutionary and radical, avant-gardist and anti-avant-gardist, attach themselves to a notion of culture as 'everyday' practice and 'everyday' practice as culture. In this light what has preoccupied Marxists and others who have written on the concept of the everyday since the Russian Revolution, is how the concept allows artistic practice and aesthetic experience to be mediated by the demands of social transformation, thereby enabling artistic practice and aesthetic experience to fall under the broader concept of cultural praxis. This is not to say that revolutionary theorists of the everyday have sought the 'politicization' or instrumentalization of the *content* of art, but rather, by bringing the alliance of culture and politics under the mantle of the everyday, the revolutionary transformation of the everyday presupposes the radical transformation of the content of social and cultural experience itself; and, therefore, by definition this process involves the transformation of the taken-for-granted market and canonic forms of culture under capitalism (its relations of production; its material and semiotic boundaries; its relationship to productive labour). Consequently, the everyday has usually been constructed and defended as the place or places where culture as the space of relations between art, aesthetic experience and labour might be reinvented in the interests of, and as part of, proletarian emancipation and the democratization of cultural production. Thus, if this notion of the everyday carries an intellectual challenge to the segregation of politics from culture, it also provides a demotic and philosophical confrontation with the categories of art and labour and the traditional accounts of aesthetic experience itself. I prefer, therefore, to think of the concept of the everyday as the very antithesis of contemporary cultural studies in this respect, insofar as it stands squarely against the discipline's disaggregation of cultural production and consumption; and – moreover, and more pertinently – for their democratic reintegration. To defend the concept today is to defend the continuing possibilities of cultural theory as a revolutionary critique of the social totality.

In this respect, *Philosophizing the Everyday*, focuses on the major *primary philosophical and political texts* which have shaped and defined the everyday as a cultural category from 1917. It does not engage with secondary sources or address itself to contemporary debates on the everyday and art. Similarly it does not concern itself with 'everyday' modes of attention or directly with the construction of the 'everyday' in early avant-garde film theory and photography, something that I have explored elsewhere.[7] To pursue these themes would dilute the wider concerns of my argument here – that, as a cultural category, the everyday is, in fact, much broader, much more capacious aesthetically and critically, than any specific art practices which might fall under its descriptions; indeed, as a cultural category it is directly subsumptive of these practices, and this is what gives the everyday its philosophical singularity. This is why I break off my historical narrative around 1975, for it is at this juncture that the debate on the concept is largely overtaken by aesthetic theory and the semiotic model of cultural studies, fundamentally transforming and narrowing its political and philosophic character. Michel de Certeau's theory of critical semiosis is a paradigmatic instance of this shift. In *Cultural in the Plural* (1974) and *The Practices of Everyday Life* (1974) he uses the phenomenological categories of memory and narrative to establish a powerful reorientation of the debate away from a general theory of cultural production to the productive consumer. Furthermore, 1975 is the point where the last great identification of the critique of the everyday with the philosophy of praxis, which had lasted for almost

20 years in the form of the Situationist International, had ended; and also the point, significantly, where Lefebvre, the key figure linking prewar and postwar debates, moves away from the direct theorization of the everyday after spending 40 years or more working on the concept. There is a sense, then, with the demise of the collective identity of the Situationist International and the rise of cultural studies in the academy, that the epoch in which the everyday had been forged through a series of richly theoretical innovations in response to an extraordinary succession of class convulsions, technological transformations, avant-garde manifestations, and forms of cultural secularization, had concluded. Consequently, in concentrating on the time span of 1917–75, we are able to link the rise and fall of the theory of the everyday across its three significant, and determining, time-lines during the twentieth century.

The first moment, of course, is the Russian Revolution itself, whose cultural, social and political impact under the auspices of modernism shattered the class-exclusions and genteel aestheticisms of the old bourgeois culture and academy across Europe and North America between 1917 and 1939. The second is the anti-Fascist Liberation in 1945 at the end of the Second World War – particularly in France and Italy – which unleashed a popular and intellectual dissent from the official forms of political restitution associated with the old prewar bourgeois ruling parties and culture. This was driven, to a certain extent, by the example and memory of the earlier prewar culture and the heroism and egalitarianism of the war years, resulting, for example, in the widespread repoliticization of realist aesthetics across all the advanced European countries. In Italy, for example, the opening up of a new cultural front between realism and modernism, exemplified by the films and writing of Pasolini and the fiction of Italo Calvino, allowed the non-Stalinist left to establish new forms of counter-hegemonic alliance.[8] And thirdly, the period of modernist counter-cultural ascendancy from 1966 to 1974, which although detached from the earlier avant-garde forms of the 'everyday' continued the revolutionary critique of high culture and political economy. This period is represented, of course, by the incendiary moment of May 1968, which transformed the post-Bolshevik form of this critique, as a generation of young non-Party intellectuals and artists withdrew their consent from all the old reformist and gradualist arguments and realist aesthetics that dominated the post-Liberation, social-democratic consensus.[9] And of all these periods, it this briefest of counter-cultural moments that has had perhaps the widest influence since.

These three time-lines – essentially covering some 50 years – are the extended historical crucible out of which the modern cultural concept of the everyday is made. In this sense there is good reason to focus our understanding of the everyday solely on these decades, because it reveals how the intellectual and culture fortunes of the critique of the everyday is bound up with an extended period of counter-hegemonic incursion into bourgeois culture during these years. It is of course easy to exaggerate the success of these incursions, just as it is easy to present a historicist procession of moments of resistance 'from below' across very different cultural milieux and social formations and mistake this for historical continuity or shared interests. In the immediate postwar period Stalinism remained impervious to the problems of cultural form. Nevertheless, taking the long view, there is something broadly unifiable about this period in the way it accomplished a decoupling of cultural production from bourgeois institutions that needs to be acknowledged and addressed in detail.[10]

In various ways, and in various modes and from various perspectives, cultural critique and the critique of capitalist forms of cultural production were in these years brought into some kind of alliance. The links between culture and the democratizing force of extra-cultural practices and interests 'from below' found various deprivatized and collective forms.

This is why it is possible to talk about the multiple counter-cultural practices in this period as mediated by something larger than their relationship to the market and the artistic canon. At various points, and in various contexts, and under various descriptions (popular and high cultural), counter-cultural practices in art, cinema, theatre and music defined their future sense of possibility from a dialogue between art and social praxis. In actuality much of what was said and done was localized in its relationship to extra-artistic forces. The working class, for example, only entered this counter-cultural world occasionally outside of the Soviet Union, and increasingly so after the 1950s with the demise of the prewar culture of radical autodidacticism and labour organizations committed to workers' education. But, nevertheless, something did thrive across class boundaries during this period. Counter-cultural practices saw themselves as orientated towards a world of everyday practices that allowed the production of art to participate in a network of social relations not defined directly by the exchange of commodities and the exclusionary interests of bourgeois institutions. This was a period of cultural groups and artist collectives, free associations and free exchanges – particularly between artists and non-artists. After 1974, and the long boom, the capitalist state, however, went on the offensive, first fitfully and hopefully, then more confidently in the 1980s and since the early 1990s, systematically and brutally stripping the public realm of the public content of this long and vital period of counter-cultural resistance. The residual counter-cultural spaces for labour, for neo-avant-garde art, and for non-bourgeois lifestyles (and realism), were gradually foreclosed or pushed out, as access to culture was recommodified as 'late modernism' then 'postmodernism'. However, this is not to say that this counter-hegemonic content was, in any ideologically precise sense, the primary target of the post-1970s capitalist cultural 'restitution', although many conservatives were enraged by how far liberationist and avant-garde rhetoric had penetrated education and cultural institutions. But, rather, the restitution was the result of capital's need to dismantle the revived militancy of labour between 1966 and 1974 and the socialized and non-market spaces and cultural interests attached to such militancy, in an attempt to restore (previous) levels of profit and the social hegemony of the bourgeoisie. This direct attack on labour and the expansion and deepening of market relations, then, was the spur to the 'reprivatization' of public culture, and more generally to the creation of a culture of dissociation between art, labour and counter-cultural form. This was characterized by the re-emergence of the power of the new liberal cultural institution after 1975, reflected, for example, in the massive museum-building programme undertaken by private and public capital by numerous states across the globe. Art and the everyday were repoliced through national forms of cultural aspiration and aesthetic, market driven, pluralism. One of the outcomes of the dissociation between art and counter-cultural form for artists was the generalized subordination of cultural praxis to aesthetic discourse. Irrespective of whether the work of artists was deemed by them or others to be disaffirmative or not, its status and visibility as art would be secured solely from within the intellectual boundaries of the art institution. This was not simply a debate, therefore, about how museums direct and take charge of the production of art, that is, encourage some practices and discourage others, but about the ways in which art is brought into cultural meaning, into cultural form, in what ways art might impinge itself on the world. In this era of the hyper-museum these counter-cultural possibilities remained seriously curtailed as the drive of the market to disconnect art from the forces of extra-artistic critique pushed art further into the realms of aesthetic docility.

Yet if the everyday is irredeemably connected to a period of work and activity, which has been destroyed in practice, this is not to say that after 1975 the themes and ideals of the early concept of the everyday became unusable, or that the 'turn' to a theory of consumption in critical theory after the 1970s did not have some critical basis in earlier theoretical work. But, rather, that the philosophy of praxis, which had sustained the *longue durée* of the concept of the everyday's ideological productivity, was in a process of dissolution and crisis, and therefore, that this dissolution and crisis has to be recognized in any revolutionary retheorization of the everyday now. Indeed, Lefebvre was saying pretty much the same thing in 1961 in the second volume of *The Critique of Everyday Life*, at the point where he himself was refashioning his revolutionary commitments: 'the idea of a revolutionary transformation of the everyday has vanished'.[11] This means that in defending the revolutionary transformation of the everyday the recovery and rehistoricization of the concept needs to be made coextensive with an understanding and assessment of the blocked utopian horizons of recent political history, and the intersection of these horizons with cultural theory. There is no concept of the everyday that is inscribable outside of this history, outside, that is, of the rewriting of this history in the present.

My emphasis, in this book, therefore, is of necessity on the key theoretical texts and critical practices which have shaped the formation of the concept, because, in thinking through this would-be vanished culture, we need to be clear about how the concept of the everyday came to possess the critical character it did, and why Lefebvre, for instance, devoted so much of his theoretical energy defending it. In this respect, the rehistoricization of the concept of the everyday invokes a simple question: what has been lost in the assimilation of the concept of the everyday into cultural studies after 1975 that makes the aesthetic and semiotic appropriation of the concept problematic? What is it that a concept of the everyday cannot do without from the earlier period? Which is not to say this book turns its face against contemporary cultural politics in a defence of some politically reinvigorated notion of the everyday shorn of its present enervating culturalism. The attack on the philosophical foreshortening of cultural studies is not an attack on cultural theory or aesthetic theory per se. In fact the very opposite applies: it is the very dimming of the political critique of the everyday through the assimilation of the everyday into cultural studies that weakens the possibility of both a workable politics in cultural practice and the possibility of politicized cultural theory and the revolutionary aesthetic content of the everyday. To critique the assimilation of the political into the cultural in theorization of the everyday, after de Certeau, then, is not to reify the political as authentically separate from the cultural or the cultural as a lesser form of politics. The *enculturalization* of politics is the great and abiding social transformation that the revolutionary critique and theorization of the everyday puts in place from 1917 to 1975. Rather, the issue is about how culture and politics are theorized *within* the realm of political economy, how cultural production is imagined and practised as social praxis now. For the assimilation of the everyday into popular culture of the moment divests the critique of the everyday of its specific philosophic dynamic: the relationship between the critique of the everyday and the critique of the social totality.

In this regard the concept of the everyday remains singularly valuable in mapping the philosophical and political legacy of revolutionary politics and Western Marxism. For what is largely overlooked in analysis of the early work of Lukács, Benjamin, Korsch, Gramsci, is how much the category of the everyday defines – directly or indirectly – the massive counter-hegemonic energy and achievements of the period.[12] Notions of critical praxis and the politicization of culture 'from below' are unthinkable without the democratizing and particularizing backdrop of the critique of the everyday. But, if Western Marxism avails itself of the everyday in order to disconnect cultural and political practice from the instrumentalities and positivism of orthodox Marxism, both postwar French cultural

studies, and its nemesis the revolutionary cultural theory of
Lefebvre and the Situationist International, adopt and transform
the category as the basis of a critique of orthodox Marxism
and Western Marxism itself. The everyday becomes a means of
continuing the theory of praxis by *other revolutionary means*,
so to speak.

This is why, in spite of my desire to extend the debate on
the everyday back to its early revolutionary origins – which is
essential to any overall assessment of its modern forms – it is
Lefebvre's reading of this legacy that still towers over the debate.
His writing represents a level of achievement that remains a
powerful focus of critical orientation for contemporary work,
and, as such, a source of continuing reflection on the everyday
and Marx's revolutionary legacy. This is not to say that his
theory of the everyday does not suffer from certain weaknesses
against other early theorists of the everyday, particularly
Benjamin (see Chapter 3). But overall his work allows us to
assess, in its assimilation of revolutionary theory from the
1920s, what revolutionary theory from the 1960s leaves us
with today. Quite simply, what distinguishes Lefebvre's writing
on the everyday from all competitors on the left in Europe in
the 1950s and 1960s is its refusal to bend the revolutionary
aesthetic content of Marx's critique of political economy to
Party diktats or putative scientific practice. In this Lefebvre sets
out his own scientific and cultural stall: the critique of everyday
life carries with it the 'dangerous memory' of the revolutionary
programme of Marx, that is – without fetishizing 'what Marx
actually said' – what is at stake is a Marx free from extra-
aesthetic, economistic, positivistic and bureaucratic distortions
and appropriations.[13] For Lefebvre, therefore, the work on the
everyday's recovery and reinscription must begin from what
remains qualitatively distinctive about Marx's programme, the
fact that it is the first revolutionary programme to bring the
transformation of the everyday into some phenomenological
alignment with the critique of capital. In Marx, there is no

critique of political economy, no critique of the value-form (the technical division of labour; necessary labour) without the collective aesthetic and sensuous reappropriation of everyday experience. The status of the aesthetic, then, is quite distinct in his writing from its position within the Romantic tradition, although of course Marx freely borrowed from this tradition. Aesthetic experience is not to be imposed on the alienations of labour or presented as a substitute for labour, but has to enter and transform the heteronomous functions of productive and non-productive labour itself. As Lefebvre puts it:

> The creative activity of art and the work of art foreshadow joy at its highest. For Marx, enjoyment of the world is not limited to consumption of material goods, no matter how refined, or to the consumption of goods, no matter how subtle. It is much more than that. He does not imagine a world in which all men would be surrounded by art, not even a society where everyone would be painters, poets or musicians. Those would still be transitional stages. He imagines a society in which everyone would rediscover the spontaneity of natural life and its initial creative drive, and perceive the world through the eyes of a painter, the ears of a musician and the language of a poet. Once superseded, art would be reabsorbed into an everyday which had been metamorphosed by its fusion with what had hitherto been kept external to it.[14]

In this respect, for Lefebvre the concept of the everyday is not an empirical category. On the contrary, the 'everyday' is a determinate abstraction, a concept in which, in Marx's sense, the pathway from the concrete to the abstract and from the abstract to the concrete enables a 'rich totality of many determinations and relations'[15] to appear. On this basis, as a cultural category the everyday is that social and experiential space in which the relations between technology and cognition, art and labour are configured and brought to critical consciousness. The space where the non-instrumental possibilities of cultural form can be tested and defended. Its theorization as a concept, as such, remains incontestably tied to the revolutionary content of its own early history: the insistence on the indivisible link between the critique of the capitalist value-form and the possibility of radically new cultural forms.

To summarize: in this book I look at the philosophical, political and cultural conflicts and contexts which have radically transformed the content of the concept of the everyday before the Russian revolution, from a term synonymous with the 'daily' and 'contingent' to one identifiable with the vicissitudes of cultural and social transformation and democratization. My aim, then, is to bring this history into focus, at a time when the revolutionary history of the concept has been all but forgotten or dismissed. In fact the current eclectic use of the term in cultural studies has severely militated against the broader understanding of the concept, delimiting the everyday's historical ties to questions of praxis, cultural form and social agency. In this respect, I want to concentrate, overall, on the two major cultural/national formations that have given ideological shape and direction to the emergence of the concept before its assimilation into cultural studies proper in the 1970s: the German–Soviet debates in Marxist philosophy and culture from 1910 to 1939, and the postwar reconstruction of the concept in the new Marxism and the arrival of cultural studies in France after the Second World War. Customarily the German–Soviet debates are written up in the histories of Western Marxism as no more than a thematic ground plan for the postwar 'invention' of the everyday.[16] Here I am interested in digging out its variegated uses, temporalities and critical lineages, in order to provide a genealogical critique of the concept's sedimented and obfuscated political and philosophical history. My point, however, is not to diminish the achievements of the postwar theorization of the everyday in France, but to problematize the part that the postwar conceptualization of the everyday has played in the general narrowing of the term.

In this regard, the identification between Lefebvre's writing on the effects of postwar commodification and consumption and the critique of everyday life is only half the story, as Lefebvre's pre-work testifies. The narrative in contemporary cultural studies in which the 'everyday' (*der Alltag*) originates in Lukács' and Martin Heidegger's early writing as a term of derogation, and is then transformed, in Lefebvre, Roland Barthes and the Situationist International, into a term identifiable with the demands of cultural and social transformation, is partial, not to say misleading. The shifts in cultural and critical usage of the term are far more complex and open to dispute than this familiar version of events would suggest.

1

The Everyday and the Philosophy of Praxis

It is only through the habit of everyday life that we come to think it perfectly plain and commonplace that a social relation should take on the form of a thing, so that the relation of persons in their work appears in the form of a mutual relation between things, and between things and persons.

Karl Marx[1]

After the Russian Revolution, the ontological marriage between 'everyday life' (*Alltag lebens*) and 'inauthentic' experience – with all its affectations of late Romantic ennui – was subject to a massive cultural and political haemorrhaging.[2] Where the industrialized everyday was once identified with that which was beneath high cultural attention or held to be bound up with limited notions of experience, it became the source of cultural renewal and political and philosophical scrutiny. This is because, above all else, the Russian Revolution destroyed the authority of the prevailing philosophical dualism of the prewar high culture in which art was forever doomed to find a purposeful cultural role in bourgeois society. The everyday was lifted out of the lebensphilosophic and neo-Romantic view of it as impersonal and mechanical and antithetical to genuine culture. Not all the neo-Romanticism of the prewar European intellengenstia was, of course, uniformly conservative or reactionary in its condescension or dismissal of the 'everyday'.

Its construction of cultural value was in part indebted to the artisanal anti-capitalism of its forebears, and as such it adopted a notional understanding of the idea of art as social critique. Indeed, where modernism had made an impact on this intelligentsia it was a modernism of the 'primitive' and the anti-industrial kind which had some influence. But the remnants of this artisanal anti-capitalism were overwhelmingly locked into a celebration of the artwork as the fount of authentic experience. The result was a failure to analyse and mediate artistic form in response to the political and social conditions of the new revolutionary and technical epoch.[3] The rise of the workers' movement, the breakdown of the prewar bourgeois formal hierarchies under the impact of modernism, the 'secularization' of culture with the increasing demotion of religious observance, and the opening up of technology in cultural production, made it impossible for defenders of neo-Romanticism to use modernism in anything but the most limited of ways as a reaction to the alienations of social experience and technology. As a result the neo-Romantic antithesis between the idea of authentic experience as inscribed in the primary judgement of of art, and the inauthenticity of alienated social experience, blocked the possibility of cultural renewal and transformation, as postwar and post-revolutionary European society sought to extricate itself from the violent collapse of bourgeois society.

Martin Heidegger and Georg Lukács were two writers who in their early work were both deeply immersed in this view of the artwork in pre-war culture, just as at the same time they both shared in a revulsion against it after the war. But, if both writers in the early 1920s took their distance from the aesthetic privations of neo-Romantic anti-capitalism (Heiddeger taking seriously Lukács' critique of the pathologies of capitalist culture), unlike Lukács, it is Heidegger who has no place for the everyday in his critical refounding of the relationship between culture and modern technology.[4] Indeed, even if the aesthetic judgement of the artwork no longer offers a space of cultural critique and subjective autonomy, the everyday remains fundamentally inauthentic. Lukács, however, reinvents himself in the wake of the Russian Revolution by embracing the *critical immanence* of everyday life. In this he identifies the limits of his early writing and the prewar artisanal anti-capitalism precisely in relation to this question of cultural dualism. In an auto-critique of his own *Lebensphilosophie* tendencies in *Soul and Form* (1910) in his post-1918 writing, he stresses the fact that the historical blockage of prewar neo-Romanticism lies in its inability to assimilate the critique of the everyday *into* the relations of production of art, thereby failing to transform the *cultural* role of art's relationship to the everyday within bourgeois society.[5] Accordingly, for Lukács it is only with Marxism and the historically unprecedented cultural praxis of the Russian Revolution that the breakdown of this dualism will be secured and the struggle for culture realized – what he had called, in a mournful tone in *Soul and Form*, the restless longing of man to 'make the pinnacle of his existence the plane on which he lives his life, to make its meaning part of everyday reality'.[6]

Lukács writing on revolutionary praxis and culture – which I will discuss in detail later in this chapter – is representative of what we might call the *post-revolutionary securalization of the everyday*: that is, the production of culture lies in the reconquest and immanent theorization of alienated, industrialized experience. This is why the breakdown of the dualism between art and cultural agency in the early post-revolutionary period also dovetails with the prewar emergence and postwar institutionalization of Freudian psychoanalysis, the other great 'secularizing' cultural force after the First World War. The grounding of human consciousness in the conflicts and disjunctions of daily life in psychoanalysis present a similar critique of philosophical dualism, but on the basis of the *desubjectivization* of the subject. The subject is recognized as the outcome of a given (and shifting) psychic history. That is, the subject's symptoms and the 'psychic disturbances of daily life'[7] are studied in relation to their discursive history and context. This brings the immanent critique of experience in Freud into a comparable position to that of the revolutionary securalization of the everyday: alienated experience becomes meaningful and purposeful experience. However, this is not to say that this denaturalization of the everyday in Freudian psychoanalysis and the denaturalization of the everyday in revolutionary Soviet cultural praxis (and early Lukács) are the same thing. Indeed, they follow very different paths culturally; and, certainly, by the late 1920s the Revolution was beginning to destroy what shared theoretical perspectives they did possess.[8] But, nevertheless, in the early 1920s for a brief period psychoanalysis and revolutionary cultural praxis converge on a shared terrain: the disinvestment of cultural theory and the human sciences from the metaphysics of tragedy.

In this respect the notion of the inauthenticity or repetition of everyday experience (as in Heidegger's notion of *Wiederholung*) undergoes two major transformations in understanding in the light of psychoanalysis and revolutionary cultural praxis in the first two decades of the twentieth century. Firstly, the radical substitution of the interpretation of *everyday speech* for neurological diagnosis in the treatment and understanding of the perturbations of psychic life and illness requires the physician actively to *listen* to the experiences of the patient thereby opening up a space for a hermeneutics of the everyday – out of silence and incoherence emerges an attentiveness to what remains hidden or partially disclosed or seemingly meaningless;[9] and, secondly, for the first time in human history the Bolshevik seizure of power is able to break the link between the collective experience of the dominated and religious and cultural fatalism, thereby allying social transformation with cultural transformation 'from below'. Thus if the denaturalization of psychoanalysis and revolutionary cultural praxis are two quite separate moments of critique with very different origins, they, nevertheless, share a similar exit from the backward-looking forms of prewar *Lebensphilosophie*, that is, they both insist on the relationality of meaning in the face of the abstractions of 'spirit' and the call to authenticity. This is why one should not underestimate the utopian content of the Russian embrace of the everyday as a cultural and social category; from 1917 the 'everyday' (*byt*) in Soviet culture is subject to an extraordinary theoretical elaboration and scrutiny that largely shapes the content of the concept through the twentieth century, pulling other uses of the 'everyday' towards it. What once was thought of as empty, featureless and repetitive, is now the source of extended collective engagement, intervention and transformation. Indeed, the very connotations of *byt* – in Russian it signifies something hard, intractable, something that presses down relentlessly on the senses – become a material and moral virtue, the imposing and necessary industrial matter that needs to be moulded and rebuilt.

The Everyday and the Machino-technical

One of the highpoints of this theoretical elaboration of *byt* is Trotsky's writing from the early 1920s in *Pravda*, first collected in English under the title of *Problems of Life* in 1924 (and republished as *The Problems of Everyday Life* in 1973).[10] In this collection, and other writings up until his exile in 1928, Trotsky returns again and again to the everyday as the focus of the achievements of the Revolution and the site where the Revolution is to be defended and deepened. As the focus of the working class's cultural and spiritual development the 'everyday' is where the revolution is to be made and remade in accordance with the new conditions of socialist construction: 'The older generation, which is more and more diminishing, learned communism in the course of a class struggle; but the new generation is destined to learn it in the elements of construction, the elements of construction of everyday life.'[11]

Here Trotsky is following Lenin's directive to the Party to shift its energies after the consolidation of power from political work to cultural work, or rather, to the transformation of political work into cultural work. 'Leninism is the knowledge and ability to turn culture, i.e. all the knowledge amassed in previous centuries, to the interests of the working masses.'[12] In this way the Revolution, Trotsky declares, unleashes a new kind of politics in which all aspects of social and cultural life are subject to evaluation and transformation. Politics are now the mediating form between the collective self-activity of the proletariat and the new cultural forms of everyday life.

> The object of acquiring conscious knowledge of everyday life is precisely so as to be able to dissolve graphically, concretely, and cogently before the eyes of the working masses themselves the contradictions between the outgrown material shell of the old way of life and the new relationships and needs which have arisen.[13]

Indeed, the disclosure of the contradictions of everyday life as the basis for new cultural forms and relations is at the very heart of what 'distinguished Marx's method'.[14]

Also exemplary of this shift of political work into cultural work in the early 1920s were Alexandra Kollantai's writings on gender, sexuality and marriage (even if the 'gendering of the everyday' was largely absent from the theorization of the concept until Simone de Beauvoir's *The Second Sex* (1949) and Lefebvre's work on femininity in the 1960s).[15] Kollantai's commitment to sexual equality and sexual liberation in a period of extraordinary ignorance and reticence on sexual questions within the workers' movement, and within the Bolshevik party in particular, directed women to the possibility of new kinds of social relationships with men and, therefore, to the transformation of the categories of everyday experience. As Trotsky himself argued in alliance with Kollantai, 'The central task in the transformation of everyday life is the liberation of women.'[16]

But, if the transformation of the everyday provided an expanded cultural space through which the revolution saw itself, this cultural space was nevertheless overdetermined by a strongly unified sense of what these modernizing conditions in the transformation of experience might actually be. The Bolshevik critique and transformation of the everyday was not an aesthetic critique of capital and political economy, it was a *technical* and *technist* transformation of pre-capitalist forms as the demand for industrialization, at Party level, overwhelmed any prospective or experimental link between the emancipation of labour, gender relations and aesthetic discourse. In this all aspects of the transformation of everyday life – the critique of bourgeois high culture, artisanal cultural practices, religion, prevailing gender relations – were officially mediated through this industrial, modernizing imperative and machino-technical culture. In Kollantai, for instance, underlying her call for sexual liberation at certain points is an almost brutal commitment to the free availability of women's bodies, as if pleasure itself had to be subject to quantifiable levels of sexual promiscuity in order for the boundaries of bourgeois morality to dissolve.[17] As such, Lenin's, Trotsky's and Kollantai's cultural politics are far from being free of the instrumental directives of what many leading Bolsheviks cited approvingly as the Americanization or Taylorization of the Revolution. Indeed, although Lenin and Trotsky diverge on what the politicization of culture might entail under this imperative – Trotsky and Kollantai being far more sympathetic to modernism – they were perhaps its most vocal defenders. Lenin sees the first responsibility of the politicization of culture as the development of class consciousness and identity through the discipline of industrial labour.[18] He is largely indifferent, therefore, in fact antagonistic, to any arguments that would weaken the refoundation of industrial production and the emergence of the Soviet Union from its pre-capitalist sloth. This is why, although Lenin did not support many of the extreme proletarian manifestations of this machino-technical culture, he nevertheless shared in its ruling spirit. Trotsky's cultural politics in *Problems of Everyday Life*, likewise, are shaped predominantly by the machino-technical imperative. The aim of revolutionaries, he argues, should not be to smash Fordism, but to socialize and purge it.[19] Such willing technism generates a tension in his writing on the everyday that is replicated in much of the leadership: between the Leninist insistence on the proletariat as the revolutionary inheritors and guardians of the highest achievements of bourgeois culture (against ultra-leftist Proletkult nihilism) and the requirements of modernization and the formation of a new culture.

It is no surprise, therefore, that in the early years of the Revolution the writings of the American Frederick Taylor and his Soviet epigone Alexei Gastev were welcomed onto the Central Committee in the name of the rationalization of labour. Gastev was the director of the Institute for the Scientific Organization of the Mechanization of Man, which devoted itself to identifying and refining the machino-technical and temporal demands of the revolution. In this, Gastev and the Institute were preoccupied with two major issues in relation to the proletarian reconstruction of the everyday: the quality of work discipline itself – the Institute employed various time-keepers to monitor worker attendance and performance – and a science of 'revolutionary efficiency and economy' in which human movement and manual skills were measured and defined by the machinic, in order to divest the body of the worker from the bad habits of bourgeois indulgence and lassitude. One of Gastev's favourite exhortations to workers was to go to bed and get up at a fixed hour in order that they might aim at 'objective hygiene of cerebral activity'.[20] One of his favourite maxims was 'Unremitting struggle, mastery of the body'.[21] This rhetoric was easily open to ridicule and Gastev's obsessive mensuration of the revolutionary body soon fell out of favour, as its palpable anti-humanist technism came into conflict with Lenin's Marxist humanist cultural inclinations; and later, with the conservative restitution of traditional cultural forms under Stalinism.

Yet, if the Revolution's submission to Taylorism is deeply problematic, it is the machino-technical that defines the very cultural politics of the revolution, and indeed which gives it its singular and progressive character. This is why if the cultural transformation of the everyday had begun and ended with Lenin's view of the proletariat as the revolutionary conduit of the monuments of world culture, there would have been no revolutionary transformation of the everyday to speak of. The revolutionary transformation of the everyday would have simply been an act of homage to, and veneration of, the 'masterpiece', rather than a necessary and iconoclastic rupture with the social and cultural relations and images of the past. The Revolution's transformation of the everyday is caught in a visible dilemma, therefore, during its early years: it is revolutionary technism which actually defines the historical and original character of the revolution and its cultural dynamism, but it is revolutionary technism which also prepares the ground for the Revolution's future social negation. This is why the debate on the machino-technical is at its most astute in that domain where the call to labour discipline and the ideal of the machinic was less bound by Party dictates: the avant-garde. In fact, in the early 1920s Constructivist and Productivist circles were the only places where technism was subject to something amounting to an internal critique. Constructivism and Productivism were certainly in agreement with the prevailing machino-technical ethos: the revolutionary transformation of the everyday could not be made from the traditional materials, practices and processes of traditional bourgeois culture. But at the same time, the defence of the new technical resources of machino-technical culture was not an argument for the Taylorization of art. On the contrary, Constructivism and Productivism subjected the prevailing machino-technical to a different and more telling question: in what ways is the emancipation of labour from capitalist relations of production actually compatible with the machino-technical? In this, Constructivist and Productivist artists and theorists such as Alexander Rodchenko, El Lissitsky, Aleksei Gan and Varvara Stepanova asked questions of the *cultural form* that the emancipation of labour might take – as such, the political and cultural implications of these questions were very different to those proposed by the defenders of the socialist reconstruction of Fordism.[22]

It is left to Constructivism and Productivism, therefore, to assert the necessary breakdown between intellectual labour and manual labour, artistic labour and productive labour, under revolutionary culture. Both Constructivist and Productivist artists talk about the artist's participation in production as the basis for the transformation of the identity of both workers and artists, and the de-alienation of art and labour. Accordingly, what is distinctive about the avant-garde critique of culture and the everyday during the Revolution is how much it is indebted precisely to Marx's critique of the technical division of labour in contradistinction to the anti-bourgeois rhetoric of revolutionary technism. In fact what is remarkable is how little Marx's *aesthetic* critique of political economy enters the cultural debates during this period. Limited to the avant-gardist margins, the revolutionary cultural transformation of the everyday is confined, at Party level, to the demand to increase the cultural level of workers and peasants. In a society of mass illiteracy this basic requirement was an obvious priority; and Lenin and Trotsky rightly attacked those idealists elements on the left that thought this illiteracy could be transcended at will. But at the same time the encouragement of cultural uplift introduced a pervasive dualism into the political rhetoric of cultural change, in an echo of prewar cultural debates. Rationalization and discipline of labour came first, cultural transformation came second. The result was a revolution in the name of the transmutation of all values, but without any sense of this transmutation as the possible liberation of sensuous form from labour. For all Trotsky's defence of the relative autonomy of art and of modernist technique his writing did little philosophically to undermine this dualism. As such, there is remarkably little Marxist reflection on the prevailing machino-technical culture even in the anti-Stalinist classics of the period. In Trotsky's *History of the Russian Revolution* (1933)[23] and Victor Serge's *Year One of the Russian Revolution* (1930)[24] there is an attenuated understanding of how Taylorization and the mechino-technical framed and channelled everyday life and revolutionary ardour.

To my knowledge in this period it is only in *The Mind and Face of Bolshevism: An Examination of Cultural Life* (1926) by René Fülöp-Miller that the everyday, technism and cultural forms of the revolution are actually discussed, although Ante Ciliga's later extraordinary revolutionary anti-Stalinist memoir *In The Land of the Great Lie* (1938),[25] provides rich insight into the bureaucratized decay of Bolshevik anti-bourgeois rhetoric during the early 1930s. Fülöp-Miller is a half-hearted and dilettantist friend of the revolution, essentially a left social democratic with a distaste for collectivism and a penchant for spiritual homilies. Yet in a prescient fashion he identifies and attacks Taylorization and machino-techical culture on the grounds that they fail to subject capitalist relations to the full force of Marx's critique of political economy. The Bolsheviks have 'neglected everything in the doctrines of Marx that went beyond arid expediency'.[26] 'The mission of [Soviet] communism is to perfect the mechanization which is already highly developed in America.'[27] But ironically, if he confronts Taylorization he fails to recognize its cultural critique in the avant-garde, preferring to endorse the worst kind of anti-avant-garde, academic practice. Fülöp-Miller, therefore, is not much of a revolutionary guide to the cultural transformation of the everyday, but in defending Marx against Bolshevik technism he does identify a problem that was to emerge in the literature on the everyday after Stalinism: the gap between Bolshevism's machino-technical transformation of the everyday and the sensuous liberation from, and transformation of, productive labour. Indeed, this is the defining terrain of the concept of the everyday as it becomes detached from the Stalinist counter-revolution in Lefebvre's writing and the Situationists in the 1950s and 1960s.

A World to be Made: Revolutionary Technism into the Philosophy of Praxis

In the 1920s and 1930s it is the machino-technical, then, that transforms the concept of the everyday into an active cultural category. Without the machino-technical imperative the revolutionary identification and transformation of the everyday would not have existed, or would not have existed in quite the same way. This is why the left critique of Lenin's and Trotsky's revolutionary technism in Constructivism and Productivism is, in the end, continuous with the machino-technical; in the absence of this continuity the avant-garde would have simply dissolved into revolutionary gesturalism and aestheticism. As such, the machino-technical is one of the primary means by which the transformation of revolutionary politics into revolutionary cultural politics is given its dynamic focus and identity, radically transforming the tenets of orthodox Marxism.

Through the revolutionary expansion of the concept of the everyday – set in motion by the Russian Revolution – there is a widespread critical revision outside of the Soviet Union of the categories of pre-Revolution Marxist philosophy and political theory, in particular the writings of Georg Plekhanov and Karl Kautsky.[28] The orthodoxy subscribed to by Plekhanov and Kautsky is not the same in detail, but they do share along with many of the defenders of Second International Marxism of this period a number of core principles that shaped the general character of the European workers' movement: firstly, the belief that the development of human society is an evolutionary process and is determined by the development of the productive forces; secondly, that the development of these productive forces need a rational and enlightened bureaucracy to put these advances in place; and thirdly, that the encouragement of rational debate and the dissemination of the natural and social sciences within the working class is sufficient to win the working class over to socialism.

In Germany, where this thinking had its most powerful institutional base, but where also there was a sizeable intellectual and working-class opposition to this kind of thought, impact of the Russian Revolution brought about a direct confrontation with the anti-culturalism of this positivism and economism. And one of the key signifiers of this confrontation was the technist mediation of the 'everyday', particularly in the work of artists and cultural theorists such as Benjamin, where the embrace of the new technologies and modernist modes of attention generated a powerful commitment to the links between cultural practice and revolutionary thought and practice.[29] As a result, the concept of the everyday as a category of revolutionary cultural transformation is seen as one of the means of uncoupling Marxism from the stultifying evolutionary and (non-revolutionary) mechanistic social categories of orthodoxy, and, concomitantly, freeing art from the aestheticism and the atemporal principles of the bourgeois art academy.

In placing a primary emphasis on the need for the continuous development and reassertion of revolutionary agency, the Second International's pragmatist and stagist road to socialism – that the last stage of social and human development is a preceding stage for the next stage of development – is exposed as a rationalist and empiricist deviation from the practical–critical content of Marx's writing. Hence, the shift from 'materialism' to cultural politics in revolutionary technism sets out to recover the Marx that European Social Democratic Marxism after the 1880s lost or discarded, and that the Russian Revolution repositioned: Marx as the philosopher and theorist of revolution.

The philosophical critique of the naturalism, economism and gradualism of orthodox Marxism and the invention of an interventionist art of the everyday, consequently, inhabit a similar conceptual universe in the 1920s. Both link politics to revolutionary cultural practice and revolutionary culture practice to the avant-garde notion of permanent revolution. But, unlike in the Soviet Union, an emergent Western Marxism did not actually produce any substantive theories *of* the everyday. Rather, in the most influential writing of the period, the everyday signifies something like a *generalized point of attraction* for the critique of prewar Marxist orthodoxy and bourgeois science. This is because the emergent theory is driven not by the objective circumstances of revolution – and therefore with the practical problems of the 'construction of everyday life' – but by the prospects for revolutionary consciousness and revolutionary agency under capitalism. The discussion of the concept of the everyday in early Western Marxism, therefore, is more generally subordinate to the *philosophic* (and at times euphoric) reinterpretation of Marxism as a theory of revolutionary praxis. Where we find reference to the everyday, we usually find a philosophical discussion of revolutionary agency. Marx, however, did not talk about revolutionary agency as a 'theory of praxis'. This is because the concept of praxis was constitutive of his critique of the passive subject of traditional materialism (Feuerbach) and the speculative subject of Idealism, it was not something that required conceptual differentiation. But, after the Russian Revolution, it became important for revolutionaries to distinguish what was qualitatively different about Marx's concept of praxis in a world of scientistic and positivist readings of Marx. In his critique of Feuerbach, Marx defines revolutionary praxis in terms of the unity of external, material transformation and self-transformation. Both subject *and* object are transformed in a continuous and mutually determining process.[30] On this basis, in the 1920s reference to the philosophy of praxis was a way of distinguishing Marx's dynamic concept of praxis from its competitors, thereby aligning what was irreducible to the Second International version of Marxism, to the Soviet Revolution and to the interventionist character of the concept of the everyday.

In these terms, the three post-revolutionary founding texts of the philosophy of praxis, Karl Korsch's *Marxism and Philosophy* (1923),[31] Georg Lukács' *History and Class Consciousness* (1923)[32] – his farewell to a Romantic naturalization of the everyday as 'inauthentic' – and *Lenin* (1924),[33] the concept of *der Alltag* is rarely used in any direct sense and is certainly never a focus for the discussion of political practice or cultural practice, as in Trotsky's pre-exile writings. Yet these books possess a revolutionary fervour that is incomprehensible without an understanding of the everyday as one of the key mediating categories of the new revolutionary epoch East and West, and, as such, the phenomenological basis of revolutionary practice. As Lukács says in *Lenin*, invoking his prewar engagement with *Lebensphilosophie* and the everyday, 'the development of capitalism turned proletarian revolution into an everyday issue'.[34] In this respect the significance of the everyday in Europe at this point lies directly in the cultural, political and philosophical impact of revolutionary praxis on a younger generation of Marxist philosophers. Thus for Korsch and Lukács the overriding question for revolutionaries in Germany after Bolshevik power is: *What are the practical and ideological problems facing the generalization of the Soviet revolution in conditions of 'stable' bourgeois democracy?* This in turn finds its expression in a philosophical defence of the political, and, as such, a defence of the primacy of the conjunctural and the *particular:* what Lenin, following Marx, called the concrete analysis of the concrete situation.

'The preeminent aim' of revolutionary method, asserts Lukács in *History and Class Consciousness*, is 'knowledge of the present'.[35] Or, as he was to say of Lenin's achievements 40 years later, Lenin's methodology was always 'an understanding of the socio-historical particularity of the given situation in which action had to be taken'.[36]

Similarly, in Korsch the turn to the concrete takes the general form of a defence of dialectics as the 'unbreakable'[37] core of Marxism's interrelation between theory and practice, and the specific form of a critique of orthodox Marxism's 'rationalist and negative'[38] – or internally undifferentiated – theorization of social consciousness. As with Lukács, Korsch decries the hubris of orthodox Marxism which opposes the proclaimed pseudo-reality of ideologies to 'correct practice'. On the contrary, ideologies are real material forces and should be studied and contested, becoming the site of revolutionary consciousness and praxis.

> Intellectual life should be conceived in union with social and political life, and social being and becoming (in the widest sense, as economics, politics, law) should be studied in union with social consciousness in its many different manifestations, as a real yet also ideal (or 'ideological') component of the historical process in general.[39]

This means that, contrary to Second International expectations, Marxism remains a set of practical problems and initiatives, and not an a priori commitment to 'scientific method' or the anticipated fulfilment of the objective conditions of the historical process. Consequently, in the late 1920s Korsch attacks the German labour movement for reducing Marxism to no more than a heuristic principle of specialist economic investigation and systematic sociology, without immediate connection to political struggles and the problems of cultural mediation and transformation. Without the 'coincidence of consciousness and reality, a critique of political economy could never have become the major component of a theory of social

revolution'.[40] In a defence of this position in 1930 – after
he had been expelled in 1926 from the German Communist
Party (KPD) for purported ultra-leftism – he condemns the
pseudo-scienticism of orthodoxy of the time for introducing
a wholly alien passivity into Marxist theory.[41] Under Second
International Marxism, Marxism has declined, he declares,
from a revolutionary theory of society into a theoretical critique
of society. The Russian Revolution, henceforth, represents first
and foremost the restoration of revolutionary Marxism.

In this respect Korsch's philosophy of praxis confronts one
of the key philosophical trouble spots in Marxist theory in
the 1920s, which was to have such a profound effect on the
development of Western Marxism and the cultural fortunes of
the concept of the everyday: the implications of Engels' later
writing on Marx's methodological legacy in the light of the
Russian Revolution.

In *Ludwig Feuerbach and the End of Classical German
Philosophy* (1886), Engels turns to a defence of Hegel's law of
transformation – of quantity into quality – in order to critique
both mechanical materialism and the reactionary evolutionary
monism of Ernest Haeckel, in a German political context in
which simplistic evolutionary metaphors of social change were
beginning to influence the fledgling communist movement.
However, the anti-evolutionist message is ambiguous given
Engels' contradictory insistence on the subsumption of
philosophy under science, and his wholly rationalistic
defence of science marching hand in hand with the emerging
proletariat. 'The more science proceeds in a ruthless and
unbiased way, the more it finds itself in harmony with the
interests and aspirations of the workers.'[42] Yet despite this
subsumption of philosophy under science, Engels' insistence
on the importance of the legacy of classical German idealism
in Marx's writing is a defiant counter to the emerging band of
evolutionists, positivists and social catastrophists. In this way
Korsch defends Engels against his mechanistic interpreters,

who were eager to read Marx's discovery of the quantifiable tendencies of capitalism as objective laws, without any qualifying commitment to questions of social agency, class consciousness and cultural activism. In this light, Korsch is emphatic: after 1917 Marxism faces a clear choice: between its collapse into a positive science, and a return to the dialectic philosophy of Hegel. For it is only the ontological link between practice and reason in the dialectical Hegelian tradition that can guide Marxism as a 'single theoretical–practical and critical–revolutionary activity'.[43]

The importance of Hegel, then, for the philosophy of praxis in the 1920s lies in its recovery of Marx's connection to the philosophy of consciousness. For in producing a 'rationalist and negative' theorization of social consciousness, orthodox Marxism, the philosophy of praxis argues, is incapable of grasping Marx's Hegelian insistence on human beings' recognition of their own alienation as the basis for its eventual supersession. Orthodox Marxism provides no framework for accounting for the mechanisms of capitalism's power over consciousness; and as such drives an irrevocable wedge between science and ethics, class consciousness and ideology, reason and the everyday. It is no surprise therefore that the discovery of Marx's Paris Manuscripts in 1931 and their publication in Moscow in 1932 was such a fillip for this critique, and a spur to the shift under Western Marxism to cultural questions and to questions of methodology. For it provided a kind of ex post facto validation of the philosophy of praxis. That is, it allowed a return to Hegel, and the concrete analysis of the concrete situation to be mediated through the category of alienation.

In this regard, *History and Class Consciousness* is the more influential and more prescient work, for in contrast to Korsch, Lukács' return to Hegel, dialectics and the problem of social agency is at the same time a philosophical recovery of the categories of alienation and commodity fetishism. Through the theoretical elaboration of the concept of alienation,

Lukács introduces a normative standard of social critique into Marxism that in turn qualifies and nuances Korsch's more general commitment to 'revolutionary consciousness': namely, that the dehumanization of bourgeois society exists independently of any individual consciousness of its effects. The significance of this revision lies, therefore, in the theoretical unity Lukács establishes between class subjectivities and the ideological mechanisms of the capitalist division of labour – what he famously calls a process of reification. To understand why individuals fail to recognize and act on their own self-estrangement and dehumanization is to recognize how the effects of commodity fetishism appear to be identifiable *with* truth and reality; subjective experience and objective social and economic forces converge. Reification is 'the necessary, immediate reality of every person living in capitalist society'.[44]

But if the bourgeoisie as a class is indefatigably constrained by these limits, the proletariat's consciousness of itself as a commodity enables it to recognize itself in relation to capital. Thus when the worker comes to know himself or herself as a commodity through his labour, his or her knowledge becomes practical and active. 'To posit oneself, to produce and reproduce oneself – that is *reality*.'[45] From this perspective Lukács' return to Hegel is philosophically far more ambitious than Korsch's. In stressing that knowledge derives from humans becoming conscious of themselves as social beings, he turns forcefully to the Hegelian notion that it is self-knowledge which shapes and directs human emancipation. In this way, the self-understanding of the proletariat as a class, as a whole, coincides with an objective and totalizing understanding of society. Thus, for this self-knowledge to come to collective consciousness and enter revolutionary praxis and transform society 'in its entirety',[46] the proletariat must overcome, in a continuous process of struggle and revision, those forces which prevent this self-understanding from achieving its historical emergence. But this struggle is only truly possible in conditions of the proletariat's ideological 'maturity'. Until the

> objective crisis of capitalism has matured and until the proletariat has achieved true class consciousness, and the ability to understand the crisis fully, it cannot go beyond the criticism of reification and so it is only negatively superior to its antagonist.[47]

In this way Lukács' philosophy of praxis produces a far-reaching shift in the conceptualization of the everyday, comparable to that of pre-1930 Soviet cultural activism's and Trotsky's critique of mechanical materialism, directly confronting what Korsch was later to call, the 'mutual impenetrability that had hitherto prevailed between the ideological positions of Russia and of Western Communism'.[48] By incorporating the effects of the ideological mechanisms of bourgeois society into an analysis of the self-knowledge of the working class as an exploited class, his concept of reification opens up the everyday under capitalist conditions to its contradictory social essence. The everyday is neither 'inauthentic' nor 'authentic', but rather, the temporal and spatial order out of which the alienations of proletarian self-knowledge will emerge. Hence the *structural* significance of his writing for Western Marxism in its turn to the concepts of alienation and reification. The conditions of proletarian self-knowledge are brought into alignment with the expansion of exchange value into all areas of daily life.

But this immanent critique of the everyday is deeply compromised by Lukács' 'messianic utopianism'.[49] With the transformation of revolutionary praxis into a problem of revolutionary self-knowledge, Lukács treats the ideological crisis of the proletariat as a revolutionary class as the central political issue affecting revolutionary transformation. This brokers material change effectively as identifiable with a prospective change in collective consciousness, leaving proletarian intervention into the processes of social reproduction as a philosophical 'ought', or rather, as an aprioristic leap into the future.

In this respect there is an overwhelming contradiction at the heart of Lukács' philosophy of praxis and incipient theory of the everyday. Despite arguing for the convergence between ideological struggle and economic struggle, and the importance of a return to the problems of class subjectivity out of Hegel, his theory of political and cultural mediation, ironically, is actually lacking in forms of concrete specification. This is because by insisting on the class consciousness of the proletariat as the *ideal repository* of the future of humanity, the proleteriat's power to change material reality through a change in its collective consciousness is ascribed a content separate from its mediation in the forms and modalities of everyday (cultural) practice, something that Korsch, despite his weaker philosophical programme, was far more conscious of. In Lukács, a revolutionary consciousness is imputed to the proletariat on the basis of its hypostatized philosophical identity as a 'class in itself', distinct from the actual divisions of its identity as the subject of its own historical reproduction. The result is that the struggle against reification becomes dependent solely upon the proletariat achieving 'full' consciousness of its subject status, leaving the transformation of the everyday subsumed under an *abstractly embodied* theory of social agency. In this light the only concrete and practical mediation is held to be the Party. Mediation, therefore, is split between a compromised or empty everyday and the idealized consciousness of the Party. De-idealized proletarian consciousness and idealized Party confront each other across a post-revolutionary (and increasingly tragic) void.

The Everyday and the Origins of Cultural Theory

Nevertheless, Lukács' turn to the question of the 'everyday' out of Hegel's theory of alienation is propitious, inseparable as it is from the need for Marxism to reconnect its critical-practical modalities to a non-reductionistic theory of consciousness and to the cultural determinations of bourgeois power. As such, by the late 1920s the philosophy of praxis began to take on a kind of prescient anti-Stalinist status, hence its 'clandestine' value for the next wave of critique of orthodoxy in the writings of Lefebvre in France and in Antonio Gramsci in prison in Italy in the early 1930s and Walter Benjamin in Germany in the late 1920s and early 1930s. In 1961 in the foreword to the fifth edition of *Dialectical Materialism* (1940) Lefebvre is absolutely clear about what this return to Hegel and the theme of alienation implies for the critique of orthodoxy and Stalinism: the question of self-estangement allows communists to 'uncover and criticize ideological and political alienations inside socialism'.[50] *Inside socialism.* By the late 1950s the anti-Stalinist cat was finally out of the bag; the immanent critique of the everyday had now expanded to cover socialist rule itself.

In *Dialectical Materialism*, written in 1934–35, Lefebvre returns to Lukácsian and Korschian themes via his own response to the Paris Manuscripts, which appeared in French in 1933 in his own translation. The German idealist language of the Manuscripts – Schelling as much as Hegel – allows Lefebvre to discredit what he sees as the shallow economism of the official (Stalinist) Marxism on Party and class: that the transition from capitalism to socialism is part of a general evolution of the productive forces of humanity. But perhaps more significantly for our narrative, the return to the Paris Manuscripts implies a critique of Lukács himself, or rather, of the political and cultural positions that ensue from the theory of reification. As Lefebvre was to say perceptively in his *Sociology of Marx* 30 years later:

> As for G. Lukács in his *History and Class Consciousness*, the proletariat's class consciousness replaces classical philosophy. The proletariat represents 'totality' – the apprehension of reality past, present and to come – the domain of possibility – in radical negation of existing reality. Unfortunately no such historical

consciousness is to be found in the working class anywhere in the world today – in no real individual, in no real group. It is a purely speculative construction on the part of a philosopher unacquainted with the working class.[51]

Whereas Lukács 'resolves' the problem of mediation through the idealized consciousness of the Party, Lefebvre actually insists on the concrete, contradictory and everyday conditions of mediation. In other words, he sees the abstract universality of historically produced species-being as always partially realized *in* alienated, everyday existence. Alienation, in other words, is not so much the inescapable condition out of which revolutionary consciousness emerges, but the *productive and conflictual force* of this consciousness.

> Alienation is not a fixed and permanent illusion. The individual is alienated, but as part of his development. Alienation is the objectification, at once real and illusory, of an activity which itself exists objectively. It is a moment in the development of this activity in the increasing power and consciousness of man.[52]

The implications of this for a theory of the everyday are enormous, although Lefebvre himself does not build on these moves until after the Second World War (see Chapter 3). By drawing out Marx's understanding of alienation as the objective basis of the production of human production and development, Lefebvre argues that the dialectical method 'joins up again with a profound materialism':[53] a materialism, that is, which is centred on the active engagement with the conflicts and contradictions of living subjects. Thus, even though the everyday is experienced naturalistically as a universal realm of habit and custom by workers, its routinizations and repetitions are not simply the expression of dominant social relations, but the very place where critical thinking and action begins. 'We must start from man as both actual and active and from the actual process of living (which is continued and reproduced everyday).'[54]

In short, Lefebvre reconnects the Hegelian/Marxian recreation of the movement of the real to the alienated universality of everyday life, conferring on the forms of capitalist reality a material and psychological significance, which both orthodox Marxism and the bourgeois social sciences had demeaned and trivialized in their respective ways. Importantly, then, Lefebvre doesn't stop at a philosophical defence of alienation as the recreation of the movement of the real. He also extends the understanding of alienation as a productive category into one of the first theoretical outlines of a critical hermeneutics of the everyday. In the 1930s Lefebvre was no ardent admirer of Surrealism's Freudianism, but he certainly understood what its cultural anthropological approach to the art-object implied for a non-reductive cultural theory. Surrealism's hermeneutical reinscription of the socially remaindered objects of the everyday clearly opened up a space of critical alignment with Marx's theory of alienation.

> [T]he most trivial object is the bearer of countless suggestions and relationships; or refers to all sorts of activities not immediately present in it ... the most complex qualities are present in the humblest of objects, conferring on them a symbolic value or 'style'.[55]

In this he gives some cultural flesh and bones to Korsch's defence of the material force of ideologies: the most undistinguished, unprepossessing and conformist of intellectual and material objects hide various kinds of disaffirmative and dissident and utopian content. This opens up a space not only for a renewed extension of politics into cultural politics (in the face of the increasing Stalinist derationalization of the everyday and the real), but for the formation of a new kind of Marxist sociology, in which the meanings of the object of study are accorded a relative autonomy. As such, it makes Lefebvre part of a tradition within Western Marxism – which would include, in particular, the early Lukács and Walter Benjamin – that sets out to *learn* from culture, rather than simply assimilating it into theoretical practice. Lefebvre's version of the philosophy of praxis could be described, then, as the first meeting inside the communist movement between Marxism as a critique of the commodity form and Marxism as a possible cultural hermeneutics of the commodity form.

The Everyday and Culture from Below

This line of thinking, of course, was also mined and developed extensively by Benjamin; and it is to Benjamin we must turn in order to configure the increasing historical tensions within Western Marxism between the construction of the everyday as a cultural hermeneutics and the philosophy of praxis. But, first, we need to switch our focus to Italy, where the philosophy of praxis brings into view another significant set of themes that will exert a profound influence on the everyday as a cultural category – albeit at a considerable historical distance from their original political context.

When Gramsci began writing his prison notebooks in gaol in the early 1930s, he was faced with a comparable set of problems to Korsch and Lukács: how is it possible for the European proletariat to win power in conditions where the bourgeoisie is culturally dominant? What are the specific strategies required for the advance of working-class interests? However, in sharp contrast to Korsch and Lukács, his work on proletarian popular 'consent' to capitalist rule is grounded in an empirical analysis of the structures of parliamentary democracy, hence the significance of his reintroduction of the term 'hegemony' from the pre-Bolshevik Russian labour movement. But the *Prison Notebooks* (not published in Italian until the 1950s) are not just a theoretical elaboration of political strategy, they are also a philosophical critique of the legacy of philosophy of praxis itself. Gramsci's work is clearly indebted to the Hegelian 'moment of rupture' of Lukács and to the shift to the 'problem of the superstructure'. But his work on hegemony is directly designed to outstrip and displace the abstractly embodied class agency of both the ultra-leftist revolutionary putschists of the 1920s and Stalinist workerists. In the theory of hegemony Gramsci is trying to work out a theory of mediation which begins from the *actual* contradictions of living subjects and concrete objects, rather than existing as a mere philosophical postulate of 'concreteness'. Hence, he rejects any notion of a unified subjectivity, setting out aprioristically from 'the contradictory state of consciousness'.[56] In this he reopens the philosophy of praxis to what Trotsky's concept of the everyday took for granted: the critical transformation of ordinary experience and 'common sense' through the socialization of intellectual and moral values. 'Common sense is not something rigid and immobile, but is continually transforming itself, enriching itself with scientific ideas and with philosophical opinions which have entered ordinary life.'[57]

In this way Gramsci brings the philosophy of praxis back into alignment with the forms and practice of working-class culture as the continuous and communal ground of struggle with bourgeois hegemony. Ideologies of ordinary life, as Gramsci calls the everyday, have a 'psychological'[58] necessity, insofar as they organize the terrain on which these everyday struggles take place. In this respect Gramsci sets out to place the 'ambiguous, contradictory and multiform'[59] consciousness of everyday experience at the forefront of the construction of the proletariat's cultural and political ascendancy, refusing to reify working-class culture as the mere repository of science and theory. As its underwriting of early 1970s Anglophone cultural studies testifies, the power of this lies in its relocation of the concept of culture to the practices and experiences of the dominated and an extension of philosophical and intellectual enquiry beyond the professions and the academy. The upshot is a Hegelian transformation of practical reason into a new Marxist understanding of mass culture from below, a 'new common sense'.[60] Indeed, Gramsci argues that the great historical achievement of his version of the philosophy of praxis is precisely its generation of a new universal culture: 'a popular mass phenomenon, with a concretely world-wide character, capable of modifying (even if the result includes hybrid combination) popular thought and mummified popular culture'.[61]

Like Korsch, Lukács and Lefebvre, Gramsci turns to Hegelian dialectics to reintegrate politics and economics, politics and culture, into an historical account of capitalism. But, unlike his predecessors, Gramsci's reflexive emphasis on consciousness and the 'concrete' finds a level of conceptual differentiation that is not paralleled elsewhere in the Western Marxist tradition in the 1930s. It is no surprise therefore that his writing has had such a huge influence on the post-1970s construction of a 'counter-hegemonic' politics in and and outside of the academy, because his theory of hegemony appears to transform a philosophy of consciousness into the actual material components of a counter-culture and the transformation of the everyday. This 'success' though comes at a cost. For if Gramsci sets out like Lefebvre to liberate proletarian consciousness from the 'brutal objectivity' (Lefebvre)[62] of reified social relations by drawing on the contradictory character of consciousness, and the need to think of cultural transformation in terms of building alliances 'from below', he does so through a loss of dialectical tension between object and subject which is comparable to that of Lukács' position. In Gramsci the relationship between proletarian praxis and the production of knowledge is based not on the scientific theorization and institutionalization of 'correct practice', but on the pragmatic incorporation of theoretical thinking into the pre-existing social forms and conditions of workers' lives. As a result every worker is a philosopher on the basis that critical reason is emergent from an engagement with common sense and not from an identification with abstract postulates.

Despite the real practical advantages of Gramsci's theory of hegemony for a theory of cultural resistance 'from below', Gramsci's work can be seen as producing a similar over-investment in proletarian consciousness to that of Lukács, albeit from an opposite perspective: revolutionary consciousness becomes based on the strength or weakness of workers' native cunning and curiousness. But if Lukács has a weaker theory of the contradictory dynamics of class consciousness, paradoxically he has a stronger grasp of the objective determinations of class consciousness under capitalism. This is because in a direct inversion of Gramsci's position he refuses to base his theory of class consciousness on the ideas contained in actual workers' heads. On the contrary, his theory of reification is predicated on the impact of commodity society as a totalizing system of forms, values and ideas which *pre-exist* their contradictory embodiment in the beliefs and practices of individuals. In the chapter 'Reification and the Consciousness of the Proletariat' in *History and Class Consciousness*, he talks about how bourgeois society is fragmented into innumerable isolated acts of commodity exchange; of how time is frozen into a quantifiable continuum of quantifiable 'things'; of how the production process is subject to a process of mechanized disintegration and how workers are separated from their humanity; of how the specialization of skills leads to the destruction of an image of society as a whole; and, therefore, how, as capitalism reproduces itself on a continuously 'higher' level, these reified structures sink deeper into consciousness. Accordingly what distinguishes this writing from Gramsci and Korsch and others is the absolute clarity with which he sees commodity exchange as producing and reproducing certain delimited forms of consciousness. This perspective he borrows largely from prewar German Sociology.

Before the First World War the Reform Movement (*Reformbewegung*) wing of early German sociology took issue with the artisanal advocates of Romantic anti-capitalism, by identifying cultural value, for the first time, with the processes of industrial modernity. Culture was not so much a thing to be saved from the depredations of mass culture, but reorganized *for* mass culture. The modern mass-produced object was credited with replacing the shared spirit of pre-capitalist social relations back into the realm of the alienated everyday, allowing commodified culture to re-emerge under modernity as a redeemed realm of pleasure (rather than a realm of brute or banal uniformity). But, for this to remain convincing, Reform Movement sociology (Georg Simmel, Max Weber, Werner Sombart) had to bracket out the category of consumption from the alienations of labour. Indeed, in order for space to be given to the new forms of commodification, labour had to be structurally demoted in favour of the subjective 'freedoms' of consumption.

This moment of separation between production and consumption could be said to have made a comparable contribution to the origins of critique of the everyday as the post-First World War notion of revolutionary praxis itself. For, paradoxically, it is this 'emptying out' of the alienation of production in the name of the authentic enchantments and disenchantments of consumption that provides Lukács with a sense of culture as work *on*, and *within*, the commodity form. By focusing on exchange value as the primary ground of discussion of the modern experience of the commodity form, the early Lukács follows Simmel in opening up a cultural space in which the modern conditions of alienation can be mediated without condescension.[63] But, if Lukács recognizes the importance of linking the consciousness of the commodity with the commodification of consciousnessness, in order to lift Marxist cultural theory out of its turn-of-the-century positivism and economism, Lukács is deeply critical of Simmel's elevation of alienation into a full-blown metaphysical principle of modern objectivity.[64] In Simmel, alienation is based directly on the instrumental powers of modern technology, which, for him, are autonomous and irreversible. Under modernity there is no escape from the quantitative expansion of the commodity form if human needs are to be met on a mass scale. This is the 'devil's bargain' with technological objectification.

Yet if Simmel confuses alienation *with* technological objectification, it is Simmel's understanding of the impact of reified social relations on consciousness that enables Lukács to recognise the expanded place of the ideological function of the commodity-form in the formation of the subject and of class consciousness. This is why *History and Class Consciousness* was so crucial for a generation emerging from the anti-psychologistic posturing of orthodox Marxism. What Lukács brings to a confrontation with Simmel is, precisely, a theory of consciousness in which worker-as-consumer and worker-as-producer are interposed. As such, there is no theory of class consciousness without a reflection on how the would-be freedoms of consumption appear to dissolve or even supersede a sense of workers as producers – hence the centrality of the concept of reification as a way of defying simplistic notions of the realm of production as an unmediated transmission belt for class consciousness. The possibility of revolutionary praxis becomes embodied in the theoretical transformation of alienated self-consciousness.

Emphasizing capitalism as a system of disordered closure and the 'unending same' becomes crucial, therefore, in imagining the possibility of its rupture and breakdown. Gramsci's theory of 'common sense' tends, however, to dissolve the terrifying force of this pre-existing totality. It is these competing conceptions of consciousness and agency – the proletariat's innate capacity for philosophizing and reflection and the proletariat's dissolution into the forces of reification – which determine much of the subsequent theorization of the everyday within Western Marxism.

The Everyday, Space and Temporality

The remarkable expansion of methodological work on consciousness and agency within this period is effectively, therefore, a retheorization of the temporality and spatial boundaries of revolutionary praxis from within a retheorized understanding of the temporal and spatial orders of capital accumulation and capitalist social relations. The problems of class consciousness and agency are situated as a problem *internal to the subject's spatial and temporal experience of technology and the social and technical division of labour.* (What are the concepts of a new 'common sense' and reification if not antithetical spatial and temporal conceptualizations of social agency?) Hence, this is why Lukács' writings possess a primary significance for the emergent hermeneutic turn to the everyday in Lefebvre and Benjamin and postwar Western Marxism generally, despite Lefebvre's antipathy to Lukács social theory. Lukács' link between the analysis of the effects of commodity production and the temporal and spatial experiences of capitalism provides the resources for Walter Benjamin, and later Lefebvre himself, to develop a cultural sociology of modernist space and time. Indeed, the power and merit of Benjamin's writing in the 1920s and 1930s is that through the analysis of the spatial and temporal content of the new forms of technological reproduction he is able to bring the everyday into sharper phenomenological and experiential focus. For Benjamin, the everyday is not simply the place where politics becomes cultural politics, as in early Lefebvre, but the site of new forms of sensuous and affective engagement between humans and technology. That is, the everyday is inseparable from its technological mediation, and as such from the experiences of closeness, distance, repetition and disorganization.

Heidegger's Everydayness, Benjamin's Everyday

History and Class Consciousness had a tributary influence on both Martin Heidegger's formulation of the concept of 'everydayness' in *Being and Time* (1927), and the intellectual formation of the young Benjamin. Benjamin and Heidegger both took seriously Lukács' spatial and temporal critique of modernity. Yet, whereas Heidegger embraces everydayness as a surrender to the inauthenticity of the present, Benjamin builds on Lukács' immanent critique of everydayness. The opening up of the phenomenological content of everyday experience is pursued within the *antiphonal context* of Heidegger's writing on everydayness, even if Benjamin and Heidegger share a dislike of notions of historical linearity.

This distinction between the 'everyday' and everydayness, then, is more than an etymological nicety; it defines a politics. Benjamin's explicit definition of the everyday as a cultural category bridges the experience of the Russian Revolution and the conditions of European modernity, producing what amounts to a reconceptualization of Soviet avant-garde notions of the everyday as space of intervention in a European capitalist setting.

Benjamin is the first writer to import the revolutionary content of the everyday into the study of the cultural meanings and experiences of the routinized, commodified everyday of bourgeois society. In this, he is the first writer within Western Marxism to give systematic attention to the alienations of the everyday as a philosophical problem of *cultural practice*. (Lefebvre's systematic attention to cultural questions does not begin until after the Second World War.) Arising from this systematic attention to culture, the activist demands of the philosophy of praxis undergo a kind of internal rupture, in which the famous split in Marx's last thesis on Feuerbach, between praxis and philosophy, action and interpretation, is dialectically reconstituted *as* a politics of interpretation. The meaning-producing content of the phenomenology of everyday capitalist experience becomes the space *of* political critique and aesthetic interruption; the 'everyday' begins its journey out of the theory of reification and revolutionary technism into a reflection on the symbolic forms of commodified experience.

There is, in this respect, a direct inversion of Heidegger's 'everydayness' as an expression of the inauthenticity of publicness. Whereas for Heidegger 'everydayness' involves a profound 'de-severance' of Being,[65] of the subjection of Being-with-one-another to that of Being-for-others, for Benjamin the technological transformation of the everyday is also a place of shared knowledge, a place where Being-for-others and social consciousness can be created and expanded. In Heidegger the self of the everyday is mechanically dispersed into the 'they',[66] the term Heidegger uses to denote the structures and effects of modern public disclosure, interpretation and communication. In Benjamin it is made tangible *through* the experience of the collective. Consequently what Heidegger calls technology's 'conquest of remoteness'[67] is double-coded in Benjamin: on the one hand, modern technology produces an increasing diminishment of face-to-face intersubjectivity; but on the other hand, modern technology reorders the representation of space and time through the objectification of the presence of the absent 'other'. Benjamin's grasp of the social development of film and photography always holds the social consequences of these two forces in place simultaneously. That is, the technologically repetitive and mechanical forms of the everyday are also defined in terms of their powers of social connectivity. This is because for Benjamin the disclosing powers of film and photography bring the appearance of things *into* social and political consciousness.

In this regard, Benjamin's development of these powers of disclosure into a theory of the crisis of the traditional experience of culture is premised, crucially, on the loss of hierarchical distance between subject and object under conditions of mass communication and representation. Benjamin's famous concept of the loss of aura as a diminishment of cultic distance between subject and object is essentially a recognition of the critical and democratic possibilities of modernity's 'levelling and averageness' (Heidegger). This 'levelling' is heralded as bringing a new set of spatial and temporal (existential) relations to the production and reception of culture. Key to understanding this is the crucial emphasis Benjamin places on how mechanical reproduction expands the production and consumption of culture – or rather how it expands the consumption of culture as the production of meaning – thereby transforming the everyday as the mediation of experience itself. As he states in 'Fragment of Manuscript', an unpublished version of 'A Small History of Photography' written in 1931:

> If in comparison to art the photographic reduction of the original proves itself to be not only an organ of consumption, but one of production – that is to say of the new valorization of old works – then that holds all the more evidently for the reality of the everyday [*der Wirklichkeit des Alltags*]. In all areas the reproducible is on the point of placing itself at the pinnacle of the value scale.[68]

The phenomenological expansion of the everyday under mechanical reproduction brings the image of the commodity and the commodification of the image into a novel realm of interpretation. As he says of Surrealist photography: the camera 'gives free play to the politically educated eye, under whose gaze all intimacies are sacrificed to the illumination of detail'.[69] Mechanical reproduction opens the interpretative functions of the producer and spectator, developing the unconscious content of looking and reading.

In all the major essays of this period Benjamin takes the breakdown of distance between subject and subject, object and subject as the basis of a new simultaneity, microscopicity and historical heightening of vision. But crucially, this simultaneous telescoping and expansion of cognition identifies a critical shift in the relations of art's production and reception. In

'The Author as Producer' Benjamin argues that the class
differences between artists and writers and the working class
are superficial in a world of transformed skills and socialized
technologies; and therefore that artists and writers should
identify themselves as proletarians through establishing their
critical place in the relations of production of their time, just
as workers should appropriate the new technologies in their
own interests. For the Benjamin of the 'productivist years'
(1930–35) the loss of aura invites a *repositioning* of the artist
and non-professional, artist and worker, as co-participants in,
and producers of, the everyday.

Benjamin does not explicitly theorize the everyday as
a cultural category, the everyday is rather the *taken-for-
granted landscape* of his analysis of modern technological
and industrial experience; in this he uses various definitions
of 'daily life' (*täglich Lebens*), 'the daily' (*täglich*) 'everyday
life' (*Alltagsleben*) and 'the everyday' (*der Alltag*) in an ad hoc
fashion.[70] However, there are a number of references where he
focusses specifically on the critical identity of the everyday as a
consequence of his critique of art's traditional functions. And
these occur, invariably, when he is discussing or recalling the
social and cultural transformations of the Russian Revolution.
One of these references is in an interview Benjamin conducted
with the Moscow evening newspaper on 18 December 1926:
'in the USSR art serves industry and everyday life'.[71] That is,
it serves industry and everyday life, *unlike under capitalism*,
where art is dependent upon employers and the market. As is
well documented, this visit in 1926 to Russia played a crucial
part in the development of his later writings. The sense of the
everyday as free from reification prompted him on this visit
to declare that private life had been abolished. As he was to
write in the later essay 'Moscow', Russia is under the 'aegis
of the new *byt*'.[72]

Such first hand reports of the new Soviet regime played
an important part in Germany in bringing the new sense

of the everyday into cultural vision, as the achievements of Russian culture became more widely disseminated into the new documentary photography, film and literature.[73] In this, much has been made of Benjamin's links to the Productivist writer Sergei Tretyakov; little work has been done, however, on the extensive debates within Productivism and the avant-garde on the everyday, particularly in the writings of Boris Arvatov. It is his work on the everyday that places the political expectations of cultural transformation for Trotsky, and the cultural allegiances of Benjamin, in a wider intellectual context. Indeed, Arvatov is one of the great missing figures in the debate on the everyday during this period, for unlike most of his revolutionary peers and the early Western Marxists, his theoretical essays on Productivism from the 1920s (published in German as *Kunst und Produktion* in 1972)[74] actually advance a theory *of* the everyday.[75] It is not clear whether Benjamin read Arvatov, given that Benjamin's Russian was poor, although he was familiar with Tretyakov; but, there is much in Arvatov that not only locates Benjamin's concern with redrawing the spatial and temporal boundaries of art, but with the critique and supersession of the everyday itself in Lefebvre and the Situationist International.

Arvatov and the Dissolution of the Everyday

For Arvatov bourgeois culture can only decorate and supplement the real, it cannot organize it. 'Instead of socialising aesthetics, [bourgeois] intellectuals aestheticize the social environment.'[76] As a result, art has been pushed out of general social praxis. Productivist art, on the other hand, breaks with bourgeois art's fetishism of form by privileging the transformation of art into a model of scientific reflection. As science engages with hypotheses in the world of the abstract, 'so will art also retain the function of constructing hypotheses in the world of the concrete'.[77] Decoration and the representational functions of art will not lose their value, but people will have a collective control over these functions as part of a democratic culture in which the mediations of bourgeois ideology through art will disappear. In this, creativity is 'to develop experiential, elastic, multiply formed and permanently fluctuating norms, for the reconstruction' of reality.[78] Workers, artists, scientists and engineers will organize a common product, destroying the category of autonomous art. Hence it is the job of working-class revolution to dismantle the gap between artists and intellectuals as the monopoly possessors of a knowledge of beauty and aesthetics, and society as a whole. The barrier between artistic technique and general social technique will disappear. 'The whole of art must be revolutionized in such a way that artistic creativity becomes the means of organization of all spheres of life, not as a beautification, but as a reformulation which corresponds to utilitarian usage.'[79]

In this way Arvatov argues that workers, artists, writers and engineers, have to *organize* and *form* the everyday. Workers, artists, writers and engineers must be involved in 'the melting of artistic forms into the forms of everyday life',[80] a phrase, of course, that was to find its way into Benjamin's own writing. Accordingly 'the problem of the reflection of everyday life is the problem of everyday life'.[81] 'It is not the "everyday" of workers which should be portrayed on stage, but rather theatre activity must unfold in life itself.'[82] In this, artistic activity will be developed according to use and the demands of specific social tasks, eventually leaving the social needs of representational art to 'die away in a thoroughly organised, integrated social system'.[83] As such, because the revolutionary transformation of the everyday is based on its ultimate supersession as a cultural and social category, Arvatov's Productivism is far in advance of those engineers, applied artists and designers in the Party who simply wanted to raise the quality of labour. 'The everyday will disappear completely, and will be replaced by continually evolving forms of social being.'[84]

The anticipated breakdown between the formal, categorial and professional divisions of culture is something that preoccupies most of the leading left communist intellectuals and avant-garde artists of the period in dialogue with the prevailing machino-technism. Benjamin's work is at the centre of this process of radical transformation. Consequently, Arvatov's Productivism is best seen in this context as the revolutionary *systematization* of many of the non-art and anti-art moves already familiar to Benjamin through the widespread emergence of the new 'documentary' and anti-aesthetic tendencies. This debt to documentary culture is, as many commentators have noted, focused largely through Benjamin's analysis of the impact of photography and film. Less attention is given, however, to the impact of the new German documentary and proletarian writing which emerged in the Soviet Union and Weimar Republic, and, as such, to the figure of the worker-correspondent.

The worker-correspondent is as significant as the documentary photographer and the Productivist technician in the development of the cultural category of the everyday in the 1920s, insofar as he or she is seen to close down the distance between subject and object, near and far, part and whole, demanded of the new cultural modes. Worker-correspondents collected materials on the issues affecting their workplace and the wider issues of the Revolution as part of a collective culture of self-representation, although workers' 'self-representation' as a concept was never separate from the interests of the Party. Worker-correspondents, then, did not just report back on their lives and other workers as oral historians might do, but put in process the sharing of ideas as the basis for the organization of demands and for petitioning discussion with others, particularly Party officials. This release of representational energy 'from below' effectively raised the cultural level at the workplace and within the working-class generally. This is why in the *Problems of Everyday Life* Trotsky devotes a great deal of space to the theoretical elaboration of the category. In raising the cultural level of the Russian proletariat (through self-objectification), the worker-correspondent for Trotsky becomes the ideal embodiment of the revolutionary transformation of everyday life. 'The worker correspondent is receptive to everything by which the working class lives and breathes.'[85] This is quite revealing of where Trotsky saw the ideal qualities of the worker-correspondent to be: he or she should be concerned first and foremost with what is *best* in the class. Trotsky's commitment to this form of cultural transformation, therefore, was in no sense comparable to its use within the avant-garde. Although he saw the worker-correspondent as the basis for new cultural relations within the working class, unlike Tretjakov, for example, he saw no political advantage in exchanging the achievements of bourgeois culture for a 'democratization of representation' 'from below'. For Trotsky, the worker-correspondent remained at odds with the anti-bourgeois cultural drive of Proletkult. In this, Benjamin's defence of the worker-correspondent was certainly closer to Trotsky than to Arvatov and Tretjakov. Yet for Benjamin, like Tretjakov, what is culturally purposeful and progressive about the idea of the worker-correspondent is his or her liminal status: the fact that he or she operates as both a productive worker *and* a cultural worker. Indeed, the production of cultural values out of the space of, and through a reflection on, the relations of production, is what provides its qualitative revolutionary content. The convergence between manual labour and intellectual labour is key to how the avant-garde saw the transformation of the role of worker and artist/intellectual during the early years of the Revolution. In the radical translation between roles, the production of new forms of attentiveness to, and identification with the everyday forms the basis for new forms of cultural production and the revolutionary transformation of the everyday.

In this light, it was worth noting that in 1926/7, at the height of his engagement with Soviet avant-garde culture, Benjamin read Larissa Reissner's 'Im Lande Hindenberg' in the cultural/political magazine *Oktober*. Reissner's social position as a writer was as far away as anyone's might be from the conventional idea of the worker-correspondent during this period. Her upper-class origins and her well-placed Party connections put her at some distance from the nascent achievements of the proletarian worker-correspondent. In most circumstances this would have condemned her to ridicule. Yet her literary docu-reportage was widely admired for its exemplary sense of intimacy with the experiences of the (German) working class. Moreover, her witty refusal of the clichés of revolutionary commitment (at the height of stolid heroic communism) and refusal to condescend to those she was writing about generated many admirers, including Trotsky.[86] *Hamburg auf den Barrikaden: Erlebtes und Erhörtes aus dem Hamburger Aufstand* (1925), her account of the abortive Hamburg uprising in 1923, during which she lived and worked and fought alongside the German working class, became a key text in the new documentary canon.[87] There is no record of Benjamin saying anything specific about her work as a model of good practice, but it clearly would have been on his critical horizon in his thinking about what kind of cultural producer the worker-correspondent might be and what kind of cultural producers workers might be. In this respect Reissner would have been one of the new writers of the 'everyday' Benjamin was thinking of in 'The Author as Producer', if only because she had little respect for official communist cultural models and protocol. 'Gaiety, roughness and a slight intoxication in the blood are considered incompatible with the calling of a European party hack', she declared.[88]

Yet Benjamin's expansion of the concept of the everyday is not simply a consequence of the development of the objective capabilities of technologies of mechanical reproduction, but of the violent and disordering powers of the forces of production as a whole. By the early 1930s Benjamin's 'everyday' is also an everyday of continuing war and the emergence of Fascism. In this way the prospect and actuality of revolution for Benjamin is that temporal space in which the interruptive violence of the proletariat's accession to power shatters the unyielding and unending violence of political economy and bourgeois rule. In this, Benjamin inherits Trotsky's sense of the everyday as the place where politics transforms experience. But after 1922–23 – at the moment of *History and Class Consciousness* – the prospect of this sense of the everyday, as a space where this counter-violence is to be forged and bourgeois violence annealed, is visibly receding, before it is finally crushed by the international forces of reaction.

The failure of revolution in Europe, the Stalinization of the Soviet and German Communist parties, the rise of Fascism, produces a concept of the everyday that is increasingly consumed by the experience and metaphors of self-violation and trauma. Consequently, what Benjamin's writing on technology and the philosophy of praxis constellates is a concept of the everyday at the moment of its passage into the fires of catastrophe. This is why it is as much the implosive image of the catastrophic as it is the interventionist figures of the Productivist and worker-correspondent that defines Benjamin's theorization of the disjunctive and microscopic powers of photography and film, and that also shapes his later revision of the philosophy of praxis. For what photography and film's unprecedented historical verisimilitude also provides is a 'close-up' of catastrophe at the moment of its actuality. By expanding the spectator's consciousness of the temporality of the everyday through the powers of mimesis, simultaneity and disruption, photography and film reproduce the catastrophic as an experience of the everyday (of closeness). The experience of catastrophe is brought back into the experience of the everyday. The striking novelty of photography and film, then, is that they are both arts of *propinquity*. They give an unprecedented visceral and affective depth to the perception of the historical event.[89]

It is important, therefore, to recognize how the issues of propinquity, catastrophe and the everyday are conjoined in the later Benjamin through his experience of Fascism. It is what Benjamin perceives as Fascism's derealization of catastrophe through the aesthetic annulment of propinquity (spectacle) that drives his spatial and temporal dynamics of the everyday. This is why the works of Ernst Jünger exerted such a fascination for Benjamin.[90] Jünger's photo-text books of the 1930s, in which images of explosions, fires and crashes are juxtaposed with images of speed and mass production, bring an extraordinary sense of photography's modern intimacy with the catastrophes of modernity into view, but from within the deadened historical space of the same. In *Das Antlitz des Weltkrieges: Fronterlebnisse deutscher Soldaten* (1930), *Der Gefährliche Augenblick* (1931) and *Die Veränderte Welt: Eine Bilderfibel unserer Zeit* (1933), the everyday is an abyss of violent repetition, a world in which technology and the subject collide.[91]

Benjamin's Productivism, then, is neither the determinate influence on his writing on culture as some might say, nor as peripheral as others might want to believe. For, if it is impossible to get the measure of Benjamin's critique of aura without the political context and conceptual framework of Arvatov's Productivism and the machino-technical, Benjamin remained orthodox on matters of the Marxist intellectual's relationship to the legacy of bourgeois culture and to art's traditional representational functions. That is, he never aligned himself directly with the dissolution of art into functionalism; for, with the expansion of the commodity form and the rise of Stalinism and Fascism, the historical tasks of representation seemed ever greater and far too important to warrant their (premature) supersession or aestheticization. With this, the significance of Benjamin's work for our narrative lies in its point of contact

and negotiation *between* various claims on the everyday during
the 1920s and 1930s, making his writing a critical confluence
of the deepening conflict in Western Marxism between the
various defences of Marxism as a philosophy of praxis and
a hermeneutics of the everyday. Thus Benjamin's work can
be seen as bridging three different concepts of the everyday:
the critique of the everyday as the reified 'reproduction of the
immediate' (Lukács);[92] the utopian dissolution of art into the
everyday (Productivism); and the representation *of* the everyday
(the rehistoricization of everyday life). If we have addressed
the first two in some detail, we need now to elaborate on the
third, for it is the third which mediates the first, qualifies the
second, and expands the terms of reference of the everyday
itself as cultural and hermenuetical category.

2
The Everyday as Trace and Remainder

Benjamin's politicization of mechanical reproduction involves the incorporation of the 'everyday' into aesthetic experience. In this sense he recognizes how technology allows consciousness to interpret 'everydayness' as culturally significant and motivated. But if this decentres producer and spectator alike from the traditional accounts of spiritual exorbitancy in aesthetic production and evaluation, photography's aesthetic 'secularization' of everyday objects and appearance is never for Benjamin a means of justifying the technological dissolution of aesthetic form into a realm of positivistic facts. Hence his ambiguous relationship to Productivism's critique of representation and aesthetic form. Technology may make the world visible, but this visibility is never transparent. The everyday is veiled. Thus, in conditions of historical stasis, what is critically significant about photography and film is not merely their social inclusiveness, but their power to draw attention *to* the opacity of everyday appearances. Photography and film *preserve* the alienated and reified content of the everyday world. Hence Benjamin's fascination with Surrealist photography and the Surrealist *objet trouvé* (found object) and the similarities between the artist as archivist of the overlooked and forgotten and the rag-picker. The remaindered commodity demands to be interpreted and possessed aesthetically, for in re-presenting its

appearance or part of its appearance in the artwork, by giving
it aesthetic semblance, historical consciousness enters its frozen
identity. In this way the entry of consciousness into the recently
modern and superseded forms of modern, mass-industrialized
culture reveals a series of traces, points where 'after-images'
of a social order not determined by the life of the commodity
as difference-as-the-same might be glimpsed. Benjamin's
unfinished *Arcades Project* is a vast, encyclopaedic encounter
with the residues of production on these terms. Architectural
details, interior designs and furniture, fashions and technologies
from the object-world of nineteenth-century Paris become the
spurs for reflection on lost desire and modernity's dreams of
the future past.[1]

From this perspective, Benjamin is the first theorist of the
everyday to incorporate the hermeneutic possibilities of Freud's
psychoanalysis into a 'microscopic' hermeneutics of culture.
As he says in the 'Artwork' essay: 'Since the *Psychopathology
of Everyday Life* things have changed. This book isolated and
made analyzable things which had heretofore floated along
unnoticed in the broad stream of perception.'[2]

In fact, if Freud recasts the psychic life in terms of the
interpretable content of everyday speech and gesture, Benjamin
recasts cultural theory in terms of the 'hidden speech' of the
commodity and everyday appearances. Thus Benjamin's
assimilation of Freud's psychoanalysis to cultural theory is
governed by the everyday's concealment of dissatisfaction
and loss. Freud describes his archeology of the unconscious
as involving the replacement of a topographical approach
in the study of psychology with a historically dynamic one.[3]
The symptom's apparent meaninglessness is given a history.
And just as the talking-cure involves the constant revoking
of the memory of trauma and the putting of this history into
words, so Benjamin's understanding of the everyday as a
realm of alienated symptoms and signs of desire invests the
interpretative 'shock' of the re-presentation of the sign with the

power to shatter the reified 'reproduction of the immediate' and rehistoricize the everyday. Both Freud and Benjamin emphasis the asymmetry between the contents of historical life and the process of remembering and representation.

In this way, Benjamin aligns the modern detachment of aesthetic experience from its embodiment in artisanal tradition with a non-linear conception of historical consciousness. Because mechanical reproduction recovers the *image* of history and frees the consciousness of the aesthetic to range over all objects and events, aesthetic experience becomes coextensive with historical consciousness on a universal basis. The temporal experience of culture is no longer identifiable with the local experience of the singular, unique object embedded in aesthetic tradition, but with the globalizing effects of mechanical reproduction itself. As such, the montaging or recontextualization of photographic material (found or otherwise) is essentially a technique which enables the historical constellation of the image. By recontextualizing, superimposing or juxtaposing temporally and culturally disparate materials, the past is made to stand in critical proximity to the present. But more importantly, this opening up of the historical continuum through photographic and literary recontextualization detaches the critical content of the past from its naturalization as what-is-no-longer. By drawing the image of the past out of its historical slumbers, the image of the past is invoked as once having been the image of the future. The temporality of the everyday is seen, therefore, as internally complex and conflictual, rather than as teleologically settled and continuous with the past.

Benjamin's theory of history shares the same target as Lukács, Korsch and Lefebvre: Second International gradualism. But Benjamin's critique of the ideology of historical linearity at the same time breaks with Lukács' concept of proletarian agency as a futural leap out of the repetitive continuum of commodity production. This is because Benjamin does not accept that repetition simply means *repetitiveness*. Lukács' theory of reification is one-dimensional precisely because it confuses the repetition of 'everydayness' under the commodity form with the persistence of the same. For Benjamin there is no such thing as *sheer* repetition. Rather, under the dominance of the 'reproduction of the immediate', historical materialism's responsibility is always to the reiterative reworking of the past *in* the alienated present, insofar as the superseded futures of the past are embedded in the possibility of the revolutionary rupture with the present. Our experience of the past is the constant renewal of the 'possible' through the gateway of the 'after', rather than a dead continuum haunted by the dream of irrevocable difference. The production of culture and of the everyday, therefore, is always and necessarily the object made anew in the present.

On this basis, Benjamin supplies the philosophy of praxis with both a theory of the discursivity of the everyday and consequently a more complex theory of modern temporality. His unification of historical consciousness and cultural practice defines the everyday in terms of its *sedimented temporal conditions and relations*. The everyday stands at the conjunction of past *and* present, present *and* future, past *and* future. Indeed, in terms of the categories of the everyday outlined earlier, Benjamin's 'everyday' has a discontinuous tripartite structure: (1) as a space of social intervention and possible revolutionary transformation; (2) as alienated symptom; and (3) as a utopian sign. It is difficult, therefore, to talk about Benjamin's work strictly in relation to the activist priorities of the philosophy of praxis. For in his adaptation of a Freudian hermeneutics he disengages the everyday as a cultural category from questions of systematic political strategy and class agency. For all his thinking on the temporality of revolutionary transformation, he is, essentially, a theorist of how the internal conflicts of historical temporality are mediated at the level of artistic form.[4] Which means that the everyday serves a very different philosophical function in its guise as unconscious symptom and sign than in the Hegelian unification of reason and praxis in Korsch and Lukács. For the turn to the 'hidden', despised, remaindered and 'microscopic' content of everyday experience unites the everyday with what *escapes* the totalization of reason and systematic philosophy. In Benjamin's theory of the trace, therefore, we see the beginnings of the postwar distinction between the everyday as that which is *familiar* (ordinary), and the everyday as that which is *remaindered*, that which is left behind after the structured activities of science, technology and social administration have defined and regulated daily experience.

In this, Benjamin's Marxism opens its heterodox origins to another strand of German idealism: Schelling's critique of reason as an abstract system. If the central preoccupation of early Western Marxism is the reunification of Hegel's immanent critique of the real with the Marxist theory of class, in Benjamin the greater focus is on the philosophy of non-identity, and, therefore, on the limitations of Hegel's 'speculative reason' as a basis for the critique of capital and modernization. As a consequence we also see the beginnings of an alignment within Western Marxism between the philosophy of non-identity and the critique of instrumental reason.

For Schelling the philosophy of Kant, Spinoza and Hegel demonstrates an essential abhorrence of reality, insofar as the three philosophers reduce the living basis of things to a pre-given order. Whereas Hegel sees the truth of freedom in the recognition of ourselves in the 'other', for Schelling self-consciousness can never be in unity with itself. Our thinking cannot overcome identity because of the division which is at the very basis of consciousness. The 'I' is essentially practical, arising through the passions and desires of self-determination. Consequently no conceptual analysis can ever exhaust its objects of understanding; there is an excess in subjectivity which philosophical reason cannot grasp. As such, Schelling rejects the Hegelian notion that Being can be derived from a necessary preceding Idea, and sees himself as finessing Fichte's unification of reason and praxis. Freedom becomes a matter of determinate choice, not the result and development of something already immanent to Being which is revealed through conceptual understanding. As Schelling argues in the *Philosophical Inquiries into the Nature of Human Freedom* (1809), there is an 'irreducible remainder [to reality] that cannot be resolved by reason'.[5] 'The unruly lies in the depths', in an infinite breakdown of the appearance of the order and form of things.[6]

The irrational and accidental reveal themselves as necessary to the formation of Being and consciousness, and therefore operate not as the enemy of reason but as something like its internal motor. Thus Schelling rejects the Spinozian/Kantian conflation between freedom and the intellectual mastery of the passions and desires. In the operative religious language of his writing, without preceding 'darkness' and disorder creation would have no basis in reality. Disorder, non-identity, and heterogeneity produce the awakening of self-will and of meaning. For Schelling, therefore, 'darkness' or Evil is a positive perversion, insofar as where there is no struggle there is no life.

As the philosopher of the significant 'remainder', Schelling provides a useful philosophical context in which to grasp the changing political and social claims of the concept of the everyday in the 1930s. For the turn to hermeneutics of the trace in Benjamin represents the point where the theorization of the everyday as revolutionary unity of theory and practice in the philosophy of praxis passes over into the hermeneutic possession of the 'everyday'. By this, I don't mean that the concept of the everyday merely becomes an intepretative or contemplative category, faced with Stalinism and Fascism and the irrealization of workers' power. But rather, that the concept of the everyday moves into that realm we now know as politics as symbolic struggle (social transformation at the level of the sign).

The heterodox philosophical theme of the 'irreducible remainder' behind the conceptualization of Benjamin's 'microscopic' theory, therefore, is one part of a generalized aestheticization of social critique and expansion of the meanings of culture under the mounting reactionary forces of reason West and East. The aestheticization of social critique and the expansion of the meanings of culture now begin to function counterfactually against the rule of instrumental reason, in an epoch where the meeting between reason and praxis on the terrain of class struggle seems a rapidly diminishing option. If the former finds its philosophical systematization in Adorno and the Frankfurt School, the latter finds its critical development in the extraordinary effloresence of writing on the 'everyday' and culture in France after the Second World War under an expanded consumer economy. Indeed what is striking about the postwar 'reinvention' of the everyday in France is how much Lefebvre, Roland Barthes, Maurice Blanchot, the Situationists and Michel de Certeau, despite their political differences, all rework the notion of the everyday as 'irreducible remainder'. For it is the theory of the 'irreducible remainder' that is now seen, precisely, as holding onto the possibility of the critique of instrumental reason.

Lefebvre: 'La Quotidienneté' and 'Le Quotidien'

Like Benjamin, in the 1930s Lefebvre begins to recognize the importance of a phenomenological hermeneutics as way out of the abstract anthropology and proletarian identitary thinking of orthodox Marxism on questions of culture. However, if *Dialectical Materialism* and 'La Mystification: Notes pour une critique de la vie quotidienne' (1933)[7] were the first moves in this direction, the path-breaking *The Critique of Everyday Life Vol. I* (1947)[8] was the concrete development of this into a theory of culture. In *The Critique of Everyday Life*, we see the philosophical summation of his turn to culture and ideology in the 1920s and 1930s. For this is the first work of philosophical criticism of capitalist culture which assimilates the themes of Lukács and Heidegger in order to move beyond them. Lefebvre identifies something shockingly simple: with the massive industrialization and urbanization in Europe in the early part of the century the production and consumption of culture is now part of the process of capital accumulation itself. The critique of alienation, therefore, cannot be based on a model of reification which separates human practice and consciousness from the advanced technological conditions of its realization. Marxism requires a far more sophisticated account of the production and consumption of mass culture, the popular and class agency, than that subscribed to by the Manichean defenders of 'reification theory' and Party orthodoxy. In a move comparable to that of Benjamin, Lefebvre recognizes that the investment in the forms of mass culture represent the partial fulfilment of needs, and therefore are irreducible to conditions of alienated subjecthood. For Lefebvre the dialectical recovery of the everyday is inseparable from seeing the reified 'reproduction of the immediate' and human practice as combined in the contradictory actuality of mass experience.

We might say, then, that the philosophy of praxis is continued by other means in Lefevbre, insofar as Lefebvre begins to think of culture in terms of 'resistance' and critique from *within* the spaces and temporalities of an emergent culture industry. For, in contradistinction to Benjamin, the philosophical theme of the 'irreducible remainder' is not just brought to bear on everydayness through intellectual labour, but is ontologically given through the autonomous self-positing of human beings. In this sense the concept of the everyday is the name given by Lefebvre to the concrete forms of mediation of the dialectic of becoming, aligning the everyday's general detachment from philosophical condescension with Gramsci's 'common culture'.

Thus if Benjamin severs the 'everyday' from 'everydayness' and 'repetition' from 'repetitiveness', Lefebvre codifies this separation by treating 'everydayness' *as the space of historically unrealized species-being*. Hence, the everyday is not just a space of critical decoding and redemption, but also a place of active dissent from everydayness. A place where mass-mediated and industrialized everydayness is unable to completely regulate and reify the shared practices, customs, forms of resistance, self-identity and moments of subversion of a 'common culture'.

From this standpoint Lefebvre is the first writer to actually codify the everyday as phenomenologically co-present with, but conceptually distinct, from mere everydayness. Lefebvre makes a fundamental distinction between 'daily life' (*la vie quotidienne*), 'everydayness' (*la quotidienneté*) and 'the everyday' (*le quotidien*): '*le quotidien*' being the modality of social transformation and class resistance, '*la quotidienneté*' being the modality of capital's administration of atomization and repetition. For if everydayness designates the homogeneity and repetitiveness of daily life, the 'everyday' represents the space and agency of its transformation and critique. Consequently in *The Critique of Everyday Life* it is possible to see Lefebvre's conceptual differentiation of the everyday as a candidate for the missing category of mediation between subject and object in Lukács' Hegelianism. In Lefebvre the everyday is the category which *grasps* the experience of the proletariat in the process of its own self-consciousness as a class. The everyday is 'lived experience (le vécu) elevated to the status of a concept and to language. And this is done not to accept it but, on the contrary, to change it.'[9]

Thus, the everyday represents those daily forms of resistance and common culture which consciously and unconsciously generate the wider horizons of class consciousness. This is

why Lefebvre, in an echo of Trotsky, sees Marx as the first
great theorist of the everyday; and why in matters of aesthetics
Lefebvre identifies, initially, in *The Critique of Everyday Life*,
with documentary and realist practices, and only later with the
expanded theory of art as cultural praxis for which he is now
noted. For, whereas in *The Critique of Everyday Life* Lefebvre's
bad-tempered opposition to Surrealism is caught up in a 1930s
positivistic-type critique of the avant-garde (despite his debt to
Surrealism's ethnographic approach to the object), in his later
writing he is far more sympathetic to the interdisciplinarity
of the early avant-garde, bringing his hermeneutics of culture
into alignment with a quasi-Productivist notion of art as social
transformation. As he was to say 40 years later:

> The highest mission of art is to *metamorphose* the real. Practical
> actions, including techniques, modify the everyday; the artwork
> transfigures it ... Art metamorphoses reality and this metamorphosis
> returns to reality. Thus, the transformation of the world is not only
> a realization of philosophy but a realization of art.[10]

Hence, if Benjamin and Lefebvre each open up the historical
consciousness of the everyday via the failure of the everyday to
mediate the universal in the present, it is Lefebvre who turns
the 'realization of philosophy' into an explicit aestheticization
of social practice.

> Critique of everyday life encompasses a critique of art by the
> everyday and a critique of the everyday by art. It encompasses a
> critique of the political realms by everyday social practice and vice
> versa. In a similar sense, it includes a critique of sleep and dreams
> by wakefulness (and vice versa), and a critique of the real by the
> imaginary and by what is possible, and vice versa.[11]

But this should not be mistaken for a dissolution of art into
political praxis. Rather, like the Productivist Benjamin, Lefebvre
takes up an Hegelian–Lukácsian theme here: art *is* praxis,
insofar as it contributes as a form of social labour to the forms
of the world; art's realization is its realization in the world, even
if its forms seem distant from the patterns and concerns of daily

life. From this perspective, then, Lefebvre's critique of everyday life does not seek to dissolve the category of autonomous art into praxis, but rather, to extend the boundaries of praxis into aesthetic experience and aesthetic experience into praxis. But if in Benjamin's model of the everyday a hermeneutics of the trace and a Productivist model of social transformation are, at various points, discontinuous, and, as such, hermeneutics becomes a means of critical reflection on the possibilities of revolutionary culture, in Lefebvre they are co-present parts of an aestheticized praxis. The outcome is a theory of culture that places a primary emphasis on the extension of the form of the artwork and aesthetic experience into the environmental and architectural. Following the lead of Surrealism, the forms and symbols of the city are incorporated into an expanded field of reference for art and, simultaneously, the sites of the city become the actual locations of artistic practice.[12] The city is taken to be both a work of art requiring interpretation (a place where meanings are generated) and a place where art is practically realized (a place where the context of the work's staging becomes part of the work's or event's identity). Thus, for Lefebvre, the aestheticization of praxis is as much about creating extra-institutional events as significant forms of cultural intervention, as it is a theory of aesthetics. Or rather, both implicate each other, and, therefore, overlap.

The Everyday and the Ethnographic Turn

This expansion of what might be meant by the cultural and social experience of art is part of a largely dissident politicization of the everyday under the state-led modernization of French culture in the late 1940s and 1950s. Indeed, after the war there is a remarkable shift in the national focus of critical theory within Western Marxism, from the experiences of German modernization to those of France. A number of factors produce this shift: the reactionary and repressive political situation in the Federal Republic; the rapid accumulation of capital in postwar France, drawing massive investment into the rebuilding of Paris, the development of the motor industry and standardized housing; the strength of an indigenous left culture organized in alliance and dissent around a politically dominant French Communist Party (PCF), capable of explaining and analysing the cultural shocks of this rapid modernization; and a Marxist intelligentsia well placed in disseminating and expanding the dialectical content of the 'everyday' against both Stalinist denunciations of 'Americanization' and the technocratic and nationalist theorization of modernization in the new heavily funded social sciences (structuralism and *Annales* School historiography).[13] In fact it is the profound lack of interest in the conflicts and aporias of modernity in crisis in structuralism which links Lefebvre's writing in the late 1940s to Maurice Blanchot's and Roland Barthes' theory of the trace in the 1950s. For what unites these writers in the 1950s is how structuralism and technocratic defences of modernization echo each other, replicating in a very different political context many of the same philosophical issues around social agency, historical change and cultural practice which dominated Lukács', Korsch's and Benjamin's critique of Second International gradualism. In these terms the political defence of the concept everyday as a trace and remainder in conditions of capitalist expansion becomes increasingly clear in France by the 1950s: that is, the everyday is now identifiable on a historical scale with a critique of the neutral ideology and 'eventless' change of modernization itself.

As a result, the identities through which the concept of the everyday mediates its strategies of critique and intervention are transformed. In the period from 1917 to 1937 the figures of the worker-correspondent, Productivist-technician and documentarist, flâneur and rag-picker dominate the intellectual and cultural landscape of the everyday. In fact the customary opposition between the flâneur and rag-picker and the worker-correspondent and documentarist is overstated once the shared sense of cultural activity as part of a collective transformation of the everyday is taken into account. Despite the overwhelming identification of the Surrealist project with the flâneur and rag-picker, the flâneur and worker-correspondent and documentarist all share a commitment to new kinds of social attentiveness based on the new technology's elevation of the powers of serendipity and contingency (in particular the photographic snapshot). Social and cultural division, the veil of ideology, are to be exposed as much through the oblique or hidden detail uncovered by the spontaneous photographic image – that is, discovered in the act of production – as through the manipulation or staging of manifest political themes. Worker-correspondent, documentarist, flâneur and rag-picker may diverge radically on what counts as productive fields of research, but they all share a sense of the cultural producer as interventionist, interrogatory and mobile. Indeed the production of the everyday is, at one level, constructed out of a minatory challenge to the sedentary identity of the traditional studio-bound artist as it is to the Stalinist bureaucrat and bourgeois social scientist. But in postwar France, as the collective and interventionist content of the everyday undergoes its demise, or is channelled into cultic philosophical–cultural programmes, the minatory challenge to traditional cultural identities remains, but the collective ideologies on which the notions of intervention and interrogation have been built are subject to a radical revision or transformation. In fact the legacy of the worker-correspondent and documentarist are now overwhelmingly subject to the ethnographic influences of the flâneur and rag-picker, as the pleasures of ironic distance or studied withdrawal become crucial to the practices of the 'irreducible remainder'. Across the writings of Barthes, Blanchot and de Certeau, it is the serendipitous role of the cultural critic and activist that is emphasized, the figure who moves with interpretive guile and dexterity through an alien world of signs, rather than the figure who invokes the praxis of the everyday and world made anew. Indeed, with the expansion of the hermeneutic traditions of the everyday in postwar France, it is the ethnographic tendencies of the prewar concept of the everyday that becomes dominant. Yet, in contrast to Benjamin, this is largely an ethnography overridden by individualist forms of negation. The cenobite or ascetic (Blanchot), existential-provocateur (Sartre), detective–gumshoe (Barthes, de Certeau), or gangster-manque (the Situationist International) become the pervasive figures.

In the ten years between *The Critique of Everyday Life* and Barthes' *Mythologies* (1957)[14] the concept of the 'everyday' takes on an increasing identification with what postwar French modernization is compelled to disavow or derogate: the socially unassimilable, culturally liminal and insubordinate; in short, all the common pleasures and mundane realities attached to those things which modernization inevitably marginalizes or leaves behind. Hence when Barthes published his collection of short pieces on the 'mythes de la vie quotidienne française'[15] in *Mythologies*, his aim was to historicize what was judged to be beneath serious critical attention: the implicit ideological content of popular cultural activities, pleasures and pastimes. With this he makes a Benjaminian move. Whereas bourgeois culture sees significance in regulation and efficiency, he sees truth in *in*significance, his intention being to produce a critical ethnography of the new object-world of postwar France in order to return social meaning to the object.

In the long run, Barthes was uncomfortable with the Western Marxian reflexes of this strategy, preferring the safer ground of French classical culture. Nevertheless, his earlier writing is compatible with a wider tendency during this period: the turn to the popular as a means of tracing out the political and cultural forms of the everyday as a field of the significant event. Indeed it is the dispute over what counts *as* the significant event that unites the early Barthes and Lefebvre. For both turn to the 'secret' historicity of the commodity in order to counter not only the 'eventless' history of structuralism, but the 'objectless' histories of Stalinism and contemporary Hegelianism. Broadly speaking, the issue of the 'significant event' becomes a localized reworking of the earlier debate in the Second International between Marxism as a science and Marxism as a critical historiography and sociology. The failure on the part of orthodox Marxism in the 1920s to follow the interdisciplinary implications of Marx's 'Introduction to the Critique of Political Economy' (1859) led to a split between history and science, empirical research and methodology, which was reinforced, as I have already mentioned, by the largely activist interpretation of Marx's last thesis on Feuerbach in orthodox Marxism. Lefebvre's and Barthes' advocacy of the significant–insignificant event, then, is a return to the epistemological problem of *where* and *in* what forms knowledge is to be situated: in the *longue durée* and the abstractions of class struggle, or in the objects, gestures and lowly and unprepossessing acts of daily life?

In these terms the dehierarchization of the event also has its philosophical moorings in the great prewar competitor to the philosophy of praxis on the French left: Sartre's left-Heideggerianism. Sartre's transvaluation of the event as the constitutive 'building block' of human labour and freedom forms a general background against which the anthropological, sociological, existential ambitions of the new cultural writing are aligned and measured. In *Being and Nothingness* (1943) he argues that the pursuit of freedom is only conceivable from within an empirical or 'environmental' setting. Freedom cannot produce its own existence; rather, it is produced from out of a discovery and overcoming of the world's resistances. Hence we can only be free in relation to a given state of things, a determinate context, an event, a *situation*, which is negated. In this way, by introducing the facticity of space into the theorization of agency and freedom, Sartre incorporates the language of labour and material production into the philosophy of consciousness. 'Freedom implies ... the existence of an environment to be changed: obstacles to be cleared, tools to be used.'[16] Freedom is indivisible from the conscious, material transformation of nature.

Heidegger's risk of freedom from out of the inauthencity of everydayness is inverted. By establishing the coextensiveness of freedom and situation, the everyday is the space from out of which the meanings of freedom are produced and mediated. Sartre, however, has no theory of the everyday or its equivalent. *Being and Nothingness* is not indebted to any of the cultural shifts taking place in the philosophy of praxis in Germany, and it would, therefore, be wrong to recruit its existential themes to the general reorientation to the philosophy of consciousness on the left. Nevertheless, Sartre's presentation of the ontological facticity of the situation provides a comparable revision of what is perceived to be the split in orthodox Marxism between the event of historical change (class struggle) and the constellation of micro-events – the 'least-events' of historical change – from out of which such struggles are born and human desire produced and reproduced. Accordingly, it is the implied connection between the micro-event and the situation which allows Sartre's concept to find its multitudinous ways into various cultural contexts in France in the 1950s and 1960s. The concept of the situation is one of the key notions that passes into the language of the postwar theorization of the everyday, insofar as its allows the everyday to be thought spatially and existentially as the place where the struggle for freedom and autonomy is embodied. In this sense Sartre's development of the idea of freedom as freedom 'in situation' can be seen as part of the wider revival of Hegelian themes between the 1920s and the 1950s.[17]

Hegel's anti-Rousseauian insistence on freedom as grounded in the rational organization of that which is well known and familiar shares the same terrain as Sartre's notion of concrete life as confronting the subject with questions that the subject is compelled to answer. That is, for Hegel, because men and women find themselves in the world as something which is already given and formed; human will is indivisible from the transformation of specific means furnished by reality.[18] I am free insofar as I am confronted with *some* thing, *some* course of action in particular. There is little, therefore, about Sartre's notion of the 'situation' that is not familiar from the critique of Kant's deflation of empirical experience in the Hegelian, Marxian and Freudian traditions of the period. Yet Sartre's notion of the 'situation' has the salient virtue of pinpointing how the concept of the everyday is overwhelmingly a post-Kantian ethical category. Indeed, more precisely, as a fully ontic category 'freedom in situation' reveals itself as a *post-Hegelian Hegelian* category, that is only *after* Marx has rescued Hegel from condescension is the theorization of the everyday conceivable as the site of the realization of reason.

The writings of Hegel-after-Marx, and Schelling, then, confront each other in the realization of the form of the everyday during this period. Without Hegel as the dialectical repository of consciousness as sensuous practice there is no conception of situated knowledge. But there is also little possibility of the irreducible remainder in Hegel, no moment when the unfolding and subsumptive logic of thought and practice brings the singularities of 'freedom in situation' into conflict with its universalizable content. This conflict is perhaps no better reflected at the time in Simone de Beauvoir's *The Second Sex*, where the return to the philosophy of consciousness and Satrean/Hegelian situation is subject to a thoroughgoing Schellingian denaturalization. That is, 'freedom in situation' is not something most women were very familiar with in the late 1940s; the 'situation' was for many women a 'closed horizon'. 'Not only is she ignorant of what constitutes a true action, capable of changing the face of the world, but she is lost in the midst of the world as if she were at the

heart of an immense, vague nebula.'[19] In this, de Beauvoir
attacks the non-relationality of men and women's experience
in the postwar world of domesticated femininity. The failure
of reciprocity between men and women makes a mockery of
the desire to 'establish the reign of liberty in the midst of the
world of the given'.[20]

The dehierarchization of the 'event' also captures the interest
of Maurice Blanchot in the 1950s, although Blanchot's work of
the time has little connection with questions of methodology in
Marxism and soon passed through and beyond a concern with
the everyday. In 1959 in his book *L'Entretien infini*,[21] in the
section on the everyday, he responds to Lefebvre, elaborating
on the everyday's particularities. Blanchot credits Lefebvre
with having transformed Heidegger's condemnation of the
everyday as the unrelenting work of reification. In this, he
identifies with Lefebvre's immanent critique of everydayness,
its conflicted and contradictory character.

> The everyday is no longer the average, statistically established
> existence of a given society at a given moment; it is a category,
> a utopia and an Idea, without which one would not know how
> to get at either the hidden present, or the discoverable future of
> manifest beings.[22]

The everyday contains an oblique truth which always
escapes the law, or discursive knowledge. By belonging to the
'insignificant', when the everyday is lived out, it 'escapes every
speculative formulation, perhaps all coherence, all regularity'.[23]
Thus, although the everyday is banal and platitudinous, it is the
very ordinariness of the everyday which brings us back to the
spontaneity of our species-being. From this, Blanchot links the
notion of the everyday as that-which-is-remaindered to the idea
of the everyday as the place where we are *ourselves* ordinarily,
that is to the experience of anonymity. 'Nothing happens;
this is the everyday.'[24] Consequently the everyday contains a
subversive, destructive capacity: the capacity to allow us to
hide, to live without external authority and responsibility and

therefore to dissociate experience from the world of reified representations. In this, he has a very different conception of the recovery of the significant–insignificant event. For, in taking the everyday to be a place of anonymity and retreat, the 'everyday is without event'.[25] That is, as a place of escape and negation it resists representation.

It is easy to imagine the kind of subject of this metaphysics of the everyday as non-event: the male intellectual or artist sitting alone, quietly reading in a Parisian cafe, watching the daily, chaotic activity of the street as a kind of constant threat to the moment of particularity, revererie and beauty. In short Blanchot himself. In this, Blanchot's model looks forward to the critical modalities of post-structuralism. But his model also represents the privatization of the everyday as 'irreducible remainder', creating a minimalist subject of the everyday, quietist and contemplative. This is very different from the dream of 'full subjectivity' which haunts the everyday in Trotsky, early Western Marxism and Lefebvre. Indeed, if Blanchot's theory of the everyday brings forth an ecstatic subject without discernible social agency, in Lefebvre the everyday remains attached to an older Marxist humanist dream of the 'total man'. And it is the revolutionary reconceptualization of this older Marxist notion of 'full subjectivity', of course, that supplies one of the most influential readings of Lefebvre and the Hegelian notion of situated knowledge in the 1950s: the Situationists' critique of capitalist spectacle.

The Situationists and the Philosophy of Praxis

The Situationist International (1957–72) is in large part the place where the critique of the everyday and the philosophy of praxis reconnect in France in the 1950s and 1960s.[26] For what distinguishes the Situationists from other French intellectuals and writers of the period is the way the group carries over and develops many of the key themes of Lefebvre's writing on the everyday – such as the hermeneutics of space and the enculturalization of politics – but without selectively disconnecting their content from the wider framework of revolutionary class politics. Barthes and Blanchot certainly share Lefebvre's anti-structuralism, but not his interest in the everyday as a utopian site of cultural transformation; or they are engaged by it only from the most abstract of perspectives. The Situationists, on the other hand, move back beyond Lefebvre to Lukács and the ultra-leftist context of the early revolutionary debates on the everyday. In this, they connect the concept of the everyday to a quite different political tradition to that of Lefebvre: council communism and proletarian anarchism. In fact, the Stalinist, Trotskyist and social-democratic context in which the 'reinvention' of the everyday takes place in France from the 1930s to the 1960s is unceremoniously attacked and dumped in the Situationist International, placing Lefebvre himself in the group's later writing in the position of a bureaucratic or 'progressivist' defender of the everyday. This is due to what the group see as the dilution of the critique of everyday life through its Barthian semiotic and sub-Surrealist appropriation in the emerging cultural theory, and in Lefebvre's own semiotic explorations of postwar consumer capitalism.[27] Hence the uncompromising return to the early Lukács and the theme of reification in Situationist writing, particularly in Guy Debord's *La Société du Spectacle* (1967).[28]

What Debord and the Situationists approve of in Lukács is the *totalizing form* under which the analysis and critique of reification is presented – that is, the way in which Lukács' is absolute in his refusal to separate the economic from the cultural – even in the early writings where he is more favourable to the redemptive power of art. In these terms, in Debord the concept of the 'spectacle' is not defined simply as a relationship to the modern diffusion and distribution of the technologically produced image. Rather, 'spectacle' is the hypostatization of the commodity in the epoch of its totalizing penetration of the senses and subjectivity. The 'spectacle', then, is precisely the power of capital made sensuously indivisible and naturalized as 'pleasure'. As such, in a return to the Lukács of *Lebensphilosophie*, the 'society of the spectacle' is held, ultimately, to be antithetical to the very production of culture. Not because high culture is downgraded by the products of mass culture, but because of the way capital-as-image substitutes shallow and decathected experiences for 'lived' experience or the self-achieved symbols of experience. From this standpoint the critique of the everyday represents the totalizing struggle against this realm of separation: between exchange value and use value, public and private, creative or artistic labour and productive labour. As they say in one of their first codifications of the everyday, 'The Transformation of Everyday Life' (1961),[29] in the next wave of revolutionary struggle the failure to link the cultural with the political is to accept the impoverishment of everyday experience. 'The next attempt to attack capitalism as a whole will have already invented and put into practice a completely new use of the everyday life.'[30]

On this score, what marks out the Situationists is their re-radicalization of the convergence between cultural struggle and the philosophy of praxis within and beyond the traditions of Western Marxism. For if Lefebvre identifies the temporal and spatial organization of modernity as a means of theorizing the forms by which a cultural resistance and critique of capitalism might take place; and as such extends this into an expanded understanding of what is judged to be culturally significant; the Situationists identify the spatial and temporal orders of every-dayness *as* the site of cultural struggle; that is, as the actual site where the imagining of a different social order is to be enacted, what they call unitary urbanism. By unitary urbanism,

> we mean a living criticism, fed by all the tensions of the whole of everyday life ... living criticism means the setting up of bases for an experimental life: the coming together of those who want to

create their own lives in areas equipped to this end. These bases cannot be reserved for any kind of 'leisure' separated from the rest of social life ... Unitary urbanism is the opposite of any kind of specialised activity.[31]

From this perspective the everyday is neither the postponed site of revolutionary social transformation nor simply a hermeneutics of culture or an expanded theory of art, but the *politicization of interventionist cultural action itself*. Social practice and artistic practice, politics and 'lifestyle' combine, as a kind of daily insurgency – what the group famously called *situations*.

In localized acts of disruption and subversion these situations – or *gestes* – become an act of revolutionary identification and, consequently, a prefiguration of the unity of reason and creativity in 'full subjectivity'. The situation arises above the alienated and heteronomous realm of the everyday in order to link its moment of negation to the imaginary horizon of revolutionary praxis. In this the Situationists borrow much from Lefebvre's theory of the Moment (which in turn is indebted to Sartre's theory of the situation). The Moment is that non-heteronomous gesture or action that stands out from the instrumental continuum of the everyday as a critique of the totality of the moments which constitute this continuum. These moments of negation (in love, play, rest) are obviously destined to disappear and be lost to symbolization, but in their moment of risk or anticipatory fantasy they push back the boundaries of the possible.[32] At the point, therefore, where the subject makes a decision in favour of another reality, the subject produces a cut or tear in the real through which the possibility of non-heteronomous social relations flows. Thus once a choice has been made in the name of what is imminently possible against what is not possible, a window on the supersession of the everyday is opened up. In this, the production of the Moment provides the nucleus of a greater counter-symbolic unity for Lefebvre: the constellation of praxis as aesthetics as festivity. Something similar is evident in the Situationists. The situation is a way of relinking spontaneous praxis to non-mediated forms of agency and attention. But for the Situationists the situation/Moment also represents a place of cultural action and confrontation. Although these actions are not named directly as 'art', nevertheless they themselves are symbolic interventions which have an affinity with neo-avant-garde practice, and it is this which gives the theory of the Situationists an interventionist force that Lefebvre's theory of the Moment doesn't have. Lefebvre may talk about aestheticized praxis in relation to expanding the boundaries of artistic practice, but the form and strategies of such praxis remain artistically vague and therefore without any sense of relationship to an audience conversant with the neo-avant-garde (see the following chapter). As Debord says in 'Rapport sur la construction des situations', in a quite different spirit:

> The construction of situations begins on the ruins of the modern spectator ... The situation is thus made to be lived by its constructors. The role played by a passive or merely bit-part playing 'public' must steadily diminish while that played by people who cannot be called actors but rather to coin a new word, 'livers', must equally steadily augment.[33]

The *ruins* of the modern spectator. The situation becomes a way of binding the politicization of aesthetics to the language of neo-avant-garde intervention. The result is a mixture of Lukácsian Teilaktion-type 1920s proletarian spontaneitism, Lefebvre's aestheticized Productivism and early Romanticism.

These themes are developed – and modified – in the only revolutionary text written expressly on the everyday since Arvatov's *Kunst und Produktion* – Raoul Vaneigem's *The Revolution of Everyday Life* (1967).[34] Written in 1963–65, it systematizes the Situationists' critique of the everyday as the realm of spectacle and separation. In this respect, Vaneigem, closely echoing *History and Class Consciousness* and Debord, identifies various forms of spatial and temporal disjunction and compression under late capitalism: the illusion of community; the internalization of social constraint and censorship; the diminution of working-class autonomy through the integration of labour into the structures of capital; the reign of the quantitative; the dominance of linear, measured time; life lived as survival (life reduced to economic imperatives); the seductions of power; an epidemic of masochist behaviour; the equivalence of meaning; the incorporation of people's identities into stereotypes through 'the role'; and the overall increase of dead time in daily life. The book develops a range of terms and concepts that offer a practical guide to these forces of reification and alienation, and as such a philosophical basis for the critique of everyday life as the critique of identity and self-preservation. It needs to be pointed out, however, that the title is a misnomer; this was the title chosen for the English translation in the 1980s on the back of the increasing interest in the everyday and the legacy of May 1968. The original title is *Traité de savoir-vivre à l'usage des jeunes générations*. A literal translation would be *The Facts of Life for the Young Generation*.

Combining the early Romantics' defence of the aesthetic as the realm of the non-identitical with a libertarian version of early Marx (via Lukács' theory of reification) and a critical anthropology, Vaneigem sets out to revolutionize the Marxist–humanist concept of the 'total man'. For Vaneigem the Stalinist and Trotskyist appropriation of the concept has been at the expense of any plausible theory of subjectivity and human emancipation. Indeed, Marxist humanism's 'total man' has been philosophically vapid and creatively bankrupt, insofar as its function is tied to the categories of bourgeois culture and the hierarchies of the capitalist division of labour: a society of self-discipline and self-sacrifice. In this regard Vaneigem is particularly repulsed by the identical return to fatherland, family and the cult of labour in the Soviet Union and postwar France. In fact it is the Situationists' recognition of the structural symmetries between capital accumulation in the West and the Soviet Union – in key aspects Vaneigem's position is a version of the theory of state capitalism – that allows the group to systematize the critique of the everyday as a critique of identity and economic self-preservation.[35] The critique of the everyday is a critique of power or it is nothing. 'The problem facing the proletariat is no longer the problem of how to seize power but the problem of how to abolish Power forever.'[36] In these terms something historically unprecedented enters the debate on the everyday, namely that for the first time the critique of the everyday now inhabits a critique of the Marxist tradition itself, or rather its institutionalized forms in Stalinism and orthodox Trotskyism. But if this isolates the SI politically in the 1950s and 1960s, the philosophical moves which underwrite their dissension are perfectly familiar from the history of Western Marxism. This is because, like Lukács, Korsch and Lefebvre, Vaneigem and the Situationists turn to the philosophy of consciousness in order to think their way out of the crisis of the stalled proletarian revolution and the reified 'reproduction of the immediate'. And significantly it is the figure of Schelling and the concept of the 'irreducible remainder' which again haunt these revisions and translations.

Above all else, *Traité de savoir-vivre à l'usage des jeunes générations* is a defence of the autonomous self-positing subject, what Schelling calls 'activated selfhood'[37] and what Vaneigem calls radical subjectivity. 'Radical subjectivity: the consciousness that all people have the same will to authentic self-realization.'[38] This irreducibility of the subject is based on the presupposition that the subject cannot be wholly transparent to itself. I cannot have consciousness of my self-determination before I exercise it; therefore, there can be no proof of my freedom, separate from its exercise. I must already be aware of what it is to have the power of freedom. In this respect Vaneigem argues that authentic self-realization is 'locked up in everyday life',[39] through penetrating what is universally given in consciousness. What Vaneigem calls the desire for realization pushes the Schellingian theme of Lefebvre's theory of the Moment into a radically revisionist context for the everyday: that is, the critique of the everyday now becomes identifiable with the self-positing creativity of the individual.

However, this should not be confused with any valorization of art or the cultivation of the individual aesthetic life. Vaneigem certainly takes from Schelling the identification of freedom with a non-repressive form of self-conscious identity, but he does not see this as being secured through the mediations of art. Rather, the act of self-positing creative individuality is the state of spontaneous being, or being-towards-others. Thus spontaneity is not a primary state which is in need of theoretical justification or artistic mediation, but the consciousness of 'lived immediacy' – a shared pleasure in other people and things. 'Thought directed towards lived experience with analytic intent is bound to remain detached from that experience.'[40] Hence Vaneigem's revisionism. For he borrows from early Romanticism only in order to sever Romanticism's identification between freedom and art from the Marxist tradition. In this, there is a fundamental attack on mediation and representation as rationalizing and identitary, turning the critique of the everyday once again back to the anti-representational legacy of Productivism. As he says, 'The new artists of the future, constructors of situations to be lived, will undoubtedly have immediacy as their most succinct – though also their most radical demand.'[41]

The emphasis on the concrete situation as the space of self-directed transformation brings Schelling, Sartre and Hegel into conflictual alignment. But Vaneigem is not a Productivist by another name, despite this alignment of creative activity directly with social transformation and the critique of representation. His investment in 'lived immediacy' has no basis in any activist conception of the reconstruction of reality. On the contrary, Vaneigem identifies the possibility of 'lived immediacy' with the spontaneous *negation* of the social world. Hence the importance of the destabilizing pleasures of play and festivity in Situationist theory. In this way it is the disruptive 'micro-events' or least-events of everyday life which resist or disrupt the logic of the spectacle and supply the basis of authentically situated (non-mediated) knowledge: impassioned daydreams, pleasures taken in love, the sudden rush of sympathy or empathy with another, the capricious gift (the potlatch), the spontaneous act. It is the link between 'pure giving' and the critique of exchange value that is key to his theory of subjectivity. Thus, whereas Blanchot's minimalist theory of the subject reduces the ideological content of the 'irreducible remainder' of the everyday to a bare minimum, leaving its negative moment stranded politically and culturally, Vaneigem's and the Situationists' maximalist subject launches it on a journey of messianic proportions. 'The new revolutionary collective will come into being through a chain reaction leaping from one subjectivity to the next.'[42]

Traité de savoir-vivre à l'usage des jeunes générations offers three indissoluble principles of the critique of everyday life: *participation, communication and self-production*. In this, Vaneigem and the SI reconnect the critique of the everyday life to a politics of time, identifying the refusal of spectacle and separation with an emancipation from everydayness. Through the systematic reintroduction into class politics of the convergence between disalienation and 'activated selfhood' and the non-identitary, the critique of everyday is reconnected to the supersession of the *official time of consumption*.

In the 1950s this connection between consumption and dead time had all but disappeared in the euphoria of the postwar boom. Modernization was the time of arrival and rapturous celebration, and rarely that of departure and inertia. It thus places Vaneigem and the Situationists' critique of the everyday at this point far to the left of Lefebvre and the other critics of

postwar modernization.[43] For if everydayness is associated with
the theft of self-realization in the abstract in early Lefebvre,
Barthes and Blanchot, in Vaneigem and the SI the theory of
'lived immediacy' deepens and polemicizes the connection
between the critique of the everyday and the critique of
exchange value. The theory of 'lived immediacy' identifies
exchange value as the *very expropriation of experience itself*.
Under capitalism 'all we have are things to look back on and
things to look forward to'.[44] But in Vanegeim and the SI this
defence of 'lived immediacy' comes at a precipitous cost. The
valorization of the link between 'lived immediacy' and the
critique of exchange value produces a premature dissolution
of subject and object, mediation and representation. Indeed, by
the time the group broke up in 1972, very specific and pressing
questions of mediation and representation were bearing down
on the dream of 'full subjectivity': the demands of the women's
movement and the post-colonial liberation movement. The
defence of festivity actually began to seem indifferent to the
demands of the new subjects.

In broad terms Vaneigem and the SI represent the last
great moment of exchange between cultural critique and
the philosophy of praxis. They define the point where the
connection between philosophy of consciousness and class
politics begins to unravel under the deconstruction of the
subject and the rise of post-structuralism. Accordingly, there
is an important sense in which the conflict between the legacy
of Western Marxism and hermeneutics enters a new critical
phase by the mid-1970s, bringing the 'everyday' into line with
the changed expectations of cultural theory itself. For by the
time Michel de Certeau writes *L'Invention du quotidien, Vol.
1, Arts de faire* (1974) (translated as *The Practice of Everyday
Life* in 1984)[45] and *La Culture au Pluriel* (1974) (translated
as *Culture in the Plural* in 1997)[46] emergent cultural studies is
returning to Barthes in order to invent the everyday as a theory
of creative consumption.

The Triumph of the 'Irreducible Remainder'

De Certeau's work has its origins in the wider debate on the everyday and popular culture in the 1970s in France, Britain and the United States of America. In this, the central concern of *The Practice of Everyday Life* embraces what is to define the development of cultural studies proper in the Anglophone world in the 1970s and 1980s: the critique of the notion of the passive consumer of culture, a notion which was the mainstay of both 1950s sociologies of mass culture, and the Frankfurt School. De Certeau's work, consequently, can be seen as part of an emergent literature in which the cultural consumption of the many is treated as active and discriminating, supplying the framework of what is later to be called reader-response theory. De Certeau expands the self-positing creativity of the subject into a cultural-studies-type differential analysis of mass consumption and the creative consumer.

But if this locates de Certeau's theory of the everyday within the immediate political context of Lefebvre, Barthes and the Situationists, his work disconnects the philosophy of praxis from any explicit totalizing critique of capitalism. The critique of the sign, and the Situationists' notion of *détournement* (the ironic negation and re-presentation of extant cultural materials) are repositioned in de Certeau as expressly practices of semiosis. The utopian identification between a theory of semiosis and the power of the proletariat to dissolve the effects of reification is denied or suspended; the critique of the everyday is now held within the symbolic spaces of capitalism, in a kind of constant war of attrition with the effects of exchange value. In this way the dissident or subversive interpretation or use of popular forms and practices becomes a kind of *poesis*, or 'rewriting' of the dominant culture. From this perspective, de Certeau's work can be seen as an attempt to put in place a modified subject of cultural resistance: by disengaging the concept of the everyday from both the determinism of the Frankfurt School and the voluntarism of the Situationists, a politicized semiotics is attached to issues of self-representation, oral history and culture 'from below'. The result is a sophisticated version of what is to become, by the mid-1970s and the perceived failure of the 1960s avant-garde, an expanded definition of the concept of resistance for the new cultural studies: the notion of the critique of the everyday as a *recoding* and resymbolization of the signifying systems of bourgeois culture.

As with the emergent Anglophone cultural studies this recoding is based on two interrelated concepts: the notion of the 'activated' subject as the transformer or transposer of pre-existing alien or dominant forms; and the identification of the voice and practice of cultural resistance with a kind of low-level disruption of the forms and symbols of power. However, it needs to be stressed that this is not attached to any counter-hegemonic theory, proletarian or otherwise. On the contrary, de Certeau's theory of the everyday exists as a tactical insinuation of the voices and practices of the working class and marginalized into the spaces, traditions and forms of the dominating.

Alluding to military strategy – and by implication to the legacy of Gramsci's quasi-militarization of cultural struggle from below – he describes these practices as cunning ruses. 'The weak must continually turn to their own ends forces alien to them'[47] – the classic precept of guerrilla warfare. Indeed de Certeau's politicization of semiosis as a kind of low-level disruptive possession of the forms and symbols of power by the dominated is based on the military interpretation of the rhetorical arts of poaching, trickery and shadow-play – the upshot of this being that in classical theories of rhetoric the sophisticated user of language sets out to make the weaker position seem stronger. He or she 'turns the tables' on the powerful by opportunism and wit. The Ancient Greeks called this *metis* or cunning intelligence and it became one of the defining attributes of the Cynic tradition. Wisdom was defined through the ability of the individual to bend to an alien situation, feigning entrapment or discomfort; then he or she would suddenly shift position in order to escape or outsmart the opposition. In this light, de Certeau develops a theory of *la perruque* ('wig') as an exemplary model of Cynic displacement and inversion. A *perruque* is defined as a borrowing of implements or materials and time by workers on the 'job' in order to produce something clandestinely for their own creative ends. In this sense the *perruque* also has much in common with the Situationist theory of the potlatch – the object produced and distributed outside of the law of exchange. De Certeau acknowledges the connection, describing the *perruque* as part of an 'economy of the "gift"'.[48] But what distinguishes this 'economy of the gift' from the Situationists, is that the appropriation of time and materials remains hidden, and therefore no 'gift' is actually exchanged.

The Practice of Everyday Life, in this sense, presents the transformation of everyday life as a series of 'microbe-like operations'[49] of resistance and creativity by the dominated and 'non-producers' or excluded producers of culture. 'To deal with everyday tactics in this way would be to practice an "ordinary art".'[50] As such there is a significant switch in cultural focus here from Lefebvre and the Situationists, in that de Certeau's use of the concept of activated selfhood is divested of any totalizing and transcendental anti-capitalist identity. In Lefebvre and the Situationists, the turn to the Moment and the situation signify, in neo-Hegelian fashion, that the actual is also the site and the emergence of the possible (the Absolute). In de Certeau, the actual maybe stand for the possible, but it is a possible of limited horizons, a possible shorn of any transcendental content. De Certeau's extension of Lefebvre's expansion of meaningful cultural activity to the veiled significations, desires and creative intentions of would-be ordinary activities becomes the *necessarily practical* way of living in an alien and alienated culture.

Innumerable ways of fooling the other's game ... that is, the space instituted by others, characterize the subtle, stubborn, resistant activity of groups which, since they lack their own space, have to get along in a network of already established forces and representations.[51]

Thus the notion of cultural resistance and creativity, as ruses and tactical insinuation, becomes a kind of understated and continuous form of activity which the system of necessity throws up. The appropriation and reuse of the meanings of the dominating – the poaching of the forms and meanings of the powerful, the insinuation of the voice of the 'other' into the reading of the bourgeois text, the 'stealing' of time from the production process – are the inevitable daily forms which resistance and creativity take under class society, lending 'a political dimension to everyday practices',[52] such as walking, reading, decorating and cooking. For example, in an elaboration of the Situationists' Surrealist flâneur, de Certeau's walker situates the experience of the city in a self-created narrative that replaces the facades and forms of the urban environment as a source of mute power and social control with a secondary poetic, social geography; he or she 'rewrites' the oppressive surface details of the city. In this, a semantic rearticulation is performed. Walking is a potential means of opening up gaps in the symbolic continuum of the urban environment through transforming what de Certeau calls 'place' into 'space'. 'Places' indicate ideological stability and the laws of the 'proper'; 'spaces' signify what happens to these laws of the 'proper' once memorization and dream have reanimated their surfaces – they become 'space[s] of enunciation'.[53] Walking facilitates the fantastical, critical or autobiographical reordering of the city's abstract geography. To be in a place, to be in place, is to 'be other and to move toward the other'.[54]

At the cultural level, de Certeau's writing represents what was to rapidly overdetermine the concept of the everyday, not only in French social theory and philosophy, but in Anglophone cultural studies: the identification of the critique of the everyday with the tactics and politics of the 'microscopic'. De Certeau's writing is part of that massive cleavage between class and politics in social theory, cultural theory and philosophy in France in the 1970s, which was to effectively identify Marxism, collective class politics and the concepts of alienation and reification with the suppression of difference and desire. In this, de Certeau's work could be said to finally bring into systematic theoretical visibility, as a determinate *cultural practice*, the split in early Western Marxism between the philosophy of praxis and a hermeneutics of the everyday. De Certeau's 'polymorph mobilities'[55] are the obvious generic partners of Jean-François Lyotard's, Michel Foucault's, Hélène Cixous's, Gilles Deleuze's and Felix Guattari's and André Gorz's capillary politics and celebration of marginal social identities. A pertinent example of this is Guatarri's identification of the microscopic with a 'politics of experimentation that takes hold of the existing intensities of desire', in his writing on psychoanalysis and politics in the early 1970s.[56] As he was to argue in 1975, in terms which are strikingly paradigmatic of this shift for a whole generation:

> In my view there are two possible politics in relation to signification. Either one accepts it *de jure* as an inevitable effect, and expects therefore to find it at every semiotic level, or one accepts it *de facto*, in the context of a particular system, and one proposes to counter it with a generalized political struggle that can undermine it from within, in such a way as to enable all the intensive multiplicities to escape from the tyranny of the signifying over-encoding ...[57]
> [As such] I shall endeavour here to get rid of the notion of two opposing *realities*, one objective, the other subjective, and replace it with that of two possible politics: a politics of interpretation that keeps going over and over the past in the realm of the unconscious phantasy, and a politics of experimentation that takes hold of the existing intensities of desire and forms itself into a desiring mechanism in touch with historical reality.[58]

Effectively, De Certeau's celebration of the 'polymorph mobilities' of the powerless and marginal as a set of practical and unconscious moves aligns a psychoanalytic interpretation of the heterogeneity of desire with a cultural politics which focuses on the immanent criticality of everyday practices and experience. Hence by the mid-1970s it is possible to trace through this dissolution of collective politics into cultural politics, an exact reversal of Lukács' dedifferentiated, reified subject: the activated subject of resistance and a 'new common sense' is now seen as in creative and open negotiation with the conditions of his or her own alienation. 'Storytelling' becomes a kind of semiotic transformation of, and symbolic emancipation from, the brute everyday.

Without question the conceptual differentiation of the everyday makes no sense without a return to the philosophy of consciousness and a defence of activated selfhood. And this is precisely because the differentiation of the everyday from mere everydayness is inconceivable without an understanding of the reproduction of society as the reproduction of agents as *subjects*. But a contradiction arises; at the same time as the return to the philosophy of consciousness demystifies the de-agentifying, pacifying functions of orthodox Marxism, Lukács' theory of reification and later structuralism, it disaggregates the collective claims of working-class agency itself in the name of an individuated cultural resistance to reification and 'dominant ideology'. In this way the critical postwar transformation of a hermeneutics of the everyday out of the philosophy of praxis, coexists in de Certeau with the wider depoliticization of the alliance between the critique of the everyday and a microscopic politics of desire in post-1968 French culture. For whatever advance is made by way of the defence of the dedifferentiation of the 'passive' subject of late capitalist mass culture is accompanied by the parcelling out of resistance to multifarious cultural acts of resistance; a politics of feints, dodges, veiling and ludic subversion. De Certeau repositions working-class resistance within the Cynic tradition.

Nevertheless de Certeau's work on consumption as enunciation and cultural production as everyday practice is instructive in one important respect: it ups the ante on the codification of the everyday as remainder through a kind of uncompromising reversal of the strictures of the Frankfurt School and structuralism. If in Adorno and Horkeimer there is no significant – *praxiological* – remainder from the incorporation of the consumer into mass culture, in de Certeau consumption is opened up to those real knowledges, histories and memories 'from below' which are to be found in the workings of ideology and the commodity form. The consumer of mass culture or the capitalist sensorium cannot be identified repressively with the products that he or she delights in or assimilates. In this respect de Certeau's writing is in keeping with the attack at the time on the notion of the 'ordinary' as ideologically closed, and as such can be traced back in particular to the ideological position of the 'ordinary' as 'irreducible remainder' in Freud's psychoanalysis.

Freud, de Certeau and the Irreducible Remainder

For de Certeau, Freud's importance lies in the way in which contingent experiences as the signs of the unconscious overflow and disrupt the images of science fixed in their own self-transparent rationality. In the face of this, in psychoanalysis, as de Certeau puts it, we are all 'like everyone else'.[59] In this respect de Certeau uses Freud's hermeneutics of the everyday in order to position the cunning subject of resistance 'psychoanalytically' as forever outside or athwart the place in which reason, science and authority think they have the subject named and controlled as a dupe of dominant ideology and a passive consumer. Accordingly, he adapts Freud's hermeneutics of the everyday to a concept of cultural resistance 'from below', by identifying the critique of the 'passive subject' with Freud's implicit critique of the notion of 'ordinariness'. In this, de Certeau identities the emergence of a post-Freudian, post-Benjaminian concept of the everyday with the collapse of the claims of a triumphant scientific elucidation (*Aufklärung*). The 'everyday' may be the site of cultural transformation, and it may be the place where reason and praxis meet, but it also brings with it enigmas and traumas which defy representation, explanation and the operations of the symbolic order.

This critique of the idea of the everyday as a positivistic or transparent category waiting to be defined or exposed by reason is clearly what Blanchot, following Freud, means by the 'secrets' of the everyday. In de Certeau there is a similar emphasis on the subterranean character of our knowledge. 'In Freud the trivial is no longer the other (which is supposed to ground the exemption of the one who dramatizes it); it is the productive experience of the text' [of speech].[60] That is, the trivial and banal are no longer 'other' to the subject's reason, but 'internal to reason', in the sense Sartre understands the 'situation' to be *in* the subject and the subject to be in the situation. But for de Certeau the reclamation and enunciation of meaning from the 'ordinary' carries a particular political thrust. It is a properly emancipatory experience precisely for those who are in the best position to know its 'secrets': those who live largely *inside* the boundaries of the everyday: the working class and the culturally dominated and excluded. Thus the subaltern subject's autonomy begins when 'ordinary' men and women become the *narrators of their own experience*. This is why de Certeau places such an importance in his emancipatory model of knowledge on the veiled status of the 'ordinary' in psychoanalysis. In Freudian psychoanalysis there is refusal to submit to the notion that the meaning of the 'ordinary' is only possible through the mastery of its forms and logic from another place – the place of the expert or master. Freud's historical approach to the symptom allows access to knowledge on the basis of the 'expert' always being in the dark, so to speak. The analyst does not use what he or she knows already in order to establish a judgement – he or she must wait to be surprised as part of an unfolding, continuous, and in a sense unfinishable, dialogue with the analysand. The analysing discourse and the analysed object, therefore, are in the same exploratory position, given the fact that there is no place outside of the analysand's ordinary language for the analyst to interpret the symptom. Analyst and analysand must constantly run up against the limits of their language. To accept this to is to accept a model of knowledge in which master and pupil continually exchange places. Neither master nor pupil is able to speak from a position of unassailable authority over the material of analysis. But for de Certeau, this is not simply an invitation to relativism. On the contrary, the exchange of position enables the voice that speaks without formally designated authority to speak with authority, that is, to speak as a contributor to knowledge.

In these terms de Certeau attacks the privileging of the scriptural over the spontaneous and oral, a theme that was to preoccupy the return to the discussion of the voice in the literary theory of *Tel Quel* and in Derrida's wider reflections in the late 1960s on the scripto-phobia of the origins of Western metaphysics.[61] But, in de Certeau's valorization of the voice, there is actually a closer affinity here to Lefebvre's later Platonist critique of modern culture as the terrorization of metalanguage: the incessant proliferation of culture as specialist discourse and the consumption of symbols about symbols. 'A society that is founded on writing and written matter tends towards terrorism, for the ideology that interprets written traditions supplements persuasion with intimidation.'[62] In this light de Certeau conjoins late Lefebvre to early Lévi-Strauss: writing – within the Western scientific tradition – is a system of oppression.[63] The history of the humanities and the sciences is a history of specialist discourses writing the voice of the 'other' as a liberation from the other's self-opacity. Science's drive to the making-transparent of the sign operates on the critical principle that there is something important and essential expressed in the speech forms of the 'primitive' children's games, the dogmas of 'true believers', the gnomic conversations of 'ordinary' people, and so on, that such subjects are not in a position to explain objectively to themselves. Science, then, recovers the speech of the 'other' from the other's own would-be incomprehension. But if writing gives conceptual form to the speech of the 'other', it is speech, de Certeau argues – its intricate flow, its motile powers of reflection – which forces people to take up writing. Thus writing may seek to bring the voice into the text, but it cannot succeed in capturing the reflective texture and somatic drive of the voice. The voice, then, for de Certeau is that non-discursive remainder of the everyday which simultaneously prepares the ground for, and resists assimilation to, scriptural production and explanation.

In the 1970s the redemptive model of consumption and the defence of an expanded notion of culture 'from below' had a profound and progressive influence on historiography as the turn to an 'open' theory of ideology – mainly out of Gramsci – impacted on other disciplines. On this score de Certeau's own description of his work on Freud as a form of 'everyday historicity' can be seen as co-emergent with the new historiography 'from below' of the period – the replacement of normative frameworks of sociological understanding with a knowledge of uses and functions of the cultures of 'speaking subjects'; for instance, the extensive work done on the cultures of resistance in Nazi Germany in the 1970s.[64] In this writing, the critique of the everyday is coterminous with the recovery of a micrology of dissent. Accordingly, the notion of an oral historiography of the everyday 'from below' is by definition, as in psychoanalysis generally, an analysis of the *failure* of dominant ideologies: that is, a theory of how social agents live with, resist, reject or endure under duress certain practices and elements of even the most brutal, oppressive and vicious of state ideologies.[65]

If this frames de Certeau's critique of the everyday as based on a form of 'counter-storytelling', it also brings into focus an alignment within the new cultural studies between the new history 'from below' and the counter-narrativization of everyday experience.

Stories of everyday life 'from below' are seen as playing a significant part in questioning and contradicting the historical transparency and self-confidence of bourgeois culture or, in de Certeau's Foucauldian language, the society of the Panopticon. Telling stories of being-in-the-world is one of the ways in which the working-class and the dominated are held to analyse the conflicts between the reproduction of everyday life as custom and habit and the reproduction of alienated social relations as a whole. The customs of everyday life, then, sustain an immanent critique of the world, locating knowledge in the analogical, rather in the objective operations of science.[66] Essentially, de Certeau's post-Situationist cultural theory represents an extension of the politics of self-representation into a meta-critique of scientific methodology. Indeed, the traditional function of science as a process of demystification within the workers' movement is seen as being in a weak position to give moral and cultural sanction to the routines and customs of everyday experience and capitalist critique (a theme of course central to Gramsci's notion of 'common sense'). But for de Certeau the emancipatory function of this storytelling is never identified with anything other than a local and symbolic challenge to social and political power. In a move reminiscent of later cultural studies in Britain and the United States, the subaltern voice is divorced from any materialist analysis of its social base and therefore from an assessment of collective levels of class consciousness. The conditions of transmission and reception of a critical oral tradition are rendered ideologically unconstrained. Storytelling 'from below' is seldom able to achieve a hegemonic consciousness from which to shape and define a collective political practice. As a result, if the activity of the cultural critic is always being mistaken for the critical activity of the consumer in theories of the creative consumer, the social function of storytelling 'from below' is always being mistaken for the work of emancipation itself. This marks what is to become the fundamental crisis of this account of the hermeneutics of the everyday as it mutates into cultural studies in the mid-to-late 1970s: with the widespread turn to a redemptive model of ideology, the critique of the everyday is now identifiable *with* self-representation and the free creativity of the enunciating subject, setting in place the generalized inflation of symbolic questions as a way of thinking about social power separate from the critique of political economy.

From this perspective, then, it is possible to divide our history of the everyday, so far, into four major philosophical categories: (1) theories of the everyday which claim to produce a subject without remainder (Heidegger); (2) theories of the everyday which produce a messianic subject (Lukács, Debord, Vaneigem); (3) theories of the everyday which produce a subject as the embodiment of social contradictions (Gramsci, Benjamin, Lefebvre); and (4) theories which produce a subject whose agency is identified with symbolic displacement or recoding (Barthes, de Certeau).

The last three categories can, in turn, be split between a concept of the subject in atomized resistance, but collectivized momentarily at points of social crisis (Vaneigem) and a concept of the subject as part of a shifting collective of counter-hegemonic alliances (Gramsci, de Certeau). By the mid-1970s, the 'reinvention' of the everyday, however, had come to define itself in relation to the latter, divesting itself of its vanguard status and avant-garde temporality. In fact, by the mid-1970s the spatial and temporal dimensions of the critique of the everyday had contracted ontologically at the same time as they had expanded hermeneutically. The dialectical mix of the messianic, anti-representational and historical content of the everyday that I noted in Benjamin was now dissolved and heavily weighted in the direction of linking representational and semiotic questions to the problems of social transformation. Henri Lefebvre understood the implications of this dissociation between revolutionary history and hermeneutics perhaps more than most, and so in the next chapter I want to return to his writing in more detail in order to look at his work in the 1960s, when the recovery of the utopian content of the concept of the everyday began to play a part in the renewed theorization of the concept for his writing and for others. In this we can establish a clearer sense of what remained at stake politically in relation to the concept during the period of its crisis and transformation.

3
Lefebvre's Dialectical Irony: Marx and the Everyday

After the publication of *The Critique of Everyday Life, Vol. I*
in 1947, Lefebvre wrote very little on the everyday. Through
the late 1940s and 1950s he became increasingly uncertain
about the philosophical value of the concept and considered
abandoning it altogether. However, in the late 1950s his
exchanges and fitful collaboration with the emergent Situationist
International changed this state of affairs, as did his final and
irrecovable split with the PCF – which had always looked
down condescendingly on his heterodox cultural interests – in
1958, after 30 years as a member. The revolutionary content
of the concept of the everyday again seemed a worthy object
of defence. In this light, in a period of exuberant creativity, he
published what amounted to a trilogy on the everyday: *Critique
de la vie quotidienne, Vol. II: Fondements d'une sociologie de
la quotidienneté* (1961), *Introduction a la modernité* (1962)
and *De la vie quotidienne dans le monde moderne* (1968),
along with a methodological defence of Marx, *Sociologie de
Marx* (1966), reprising a number of the themes of *Dialectical
Materialism*.[1] In 1960 he also founded the 'Research Group
on everyday life' at the Centre d'études sociologiques (CES),
where he was then employed.

The three volumes on the everyday amount to a massive
expansion and redefence of his early work, but now

emboldened and deepened in their philosophical ambition by an uninhibited critique of Stalinism. In this respect, if Volume 1 of the *Critique de la vie quotidienne* represents an assessment and mediation of his formative engagement with the revolutionary culture theory of the 1920s and 1930s in a period of postwar optimism, the three later volumes on the everyday represent a defence of the concept of the everyday at the height of post-Bolshevik cynicism and the institutional rise of modernism. Consequently the three volumes are less a report back on the prospects for revolutionary cultural critique than a repositioning of the ideal of the critique of the everyday in the wake of the rapid advance of postwar consumer capitalism. As such, their production is defined by a a palpable split in form: on the one hand, by an overwhelming sense of loss of the critique of the everyday as revolutionary praxis, but, on the other hand, by a renewed theoretical energy on Lefebvre's part in the face of the dynamics of the new culture. Indeed, theoretically, the three volumes 'overtake' the earlier volume, providing an expanded framework for the analysis of alienation and the reproduction of the everyday. In this light the trilogy develops its arguments in dialogue with a number of ideological practices and philosophical materials: with the remnants of Stalinist orthodoxy – now even more entrenched in the PCF, although the Party was in ideological freefall after 1956; with the emergent postwar writing in France on the everyday (in particular Barthes); with the neo-avant-garde; with the increasing technological colonization of everyday life; and, most significantly, with the legacy of Marx's revolutionary programme itself. On this basis the three books bring the postwar critique of the everyday back into more than contemporary political focus. Rather, in an ambitious programme of anti-Stalinist reclamation, they set out to defend Marx's legacy as (one of) the unsurpassable horizons of the critique of the everyday. However, this is not simply a defence of Marxism as revolutionary praxis, but a defence of the revolutionary praxis of Marx. That is, in a rebuttal of both Stalinism and the growing demotion of Marx on the left in France, Lefebvre returns to his discussion of the early Marx of the 1930s to link the critique of everyday life with the implicit aesthetic and ethical critique of reason in Marx's programme. 'What did Marx want? What did the initial Marxist project consist of?' he asks in *The Critique of Everyday Life, Vol. II*.[2] The initial Marxist project consisted, he replies, in the transformation of everyday life as a *total revolutionary praxis*. And this total revolutionary praxis consists of two substantive and interrelated projects: the formation of a new set of ethical relations between the 'private' and public or civic realms. In this, Marx reverses Hegel's notion that it is the perfection of the state that embodies such an ethical ideal. For Marx, rather, it is only through the dissolution of the state that these ideal relations will take concrete form. The second project is the necessary aesthetic character of this dissolution. Ultimately, art, as the socially divided expression of the technical and bureaucratic conditions of culture, must disappear, and be replaced by a generalized and non-heteronomous experience of creativity. Thus, once art is superseded as an autonomous technical category, it would then be reabsorbed into the everyday, which itself would then be transformed by what hitherto had been suppressed by the reign of the commodity relations. Accordingly, the alienated powers of 'expression', 'beauty' and 'spiritual detemporalization' would journey back into the everyday in order to radically repossess what is meant by 'experience' and social relations under capitalism. In this respect, the dissolution of the state and art would combine to produce a 'total metamorphosis of the everyday'.[3]

> We will therefore go so far as to argue that critique of everyday life – radical critique aimed at attaining the radical metamorphosis of everyday life – is alone in taking up the authentic Marxist project again and in continuing it: to supersede philosophy and to fulfil it.[4]

Lefebvre's neo-Hegelianism is here at its most explicit: the critique of the everyday represents the undertaking of the *total* critique of totality. That is, the dissolution of the state and the category of art is for Lefebvre where Marx's programme becomes indebted to more than the familiar husk of Hegel's dialectical categories, but to the actual superfetation of the dialectic in the Hegelian Absolute: the negation and supersession of negation and supersession itself. 'With Hegel, extensibility in time ("becoming") comes firmly to the fore, takes on primordiality.'[5] In this sense, Marx's programme operates in the place of Hegel's Absolute – the stilling and subsumption of negation – as the revolutionary transformation of identity into non-identity or, rather, the free play of difference. Thus, Lefebvre retains enough of his Hegelianism from the 1930s to insist that the total metamorphosis of the everyday is another name for Marx's praxiological and anti-statist transmutation of the Absolute. 'Marxian thought is not merely oriented towards action. It is a theory of action, reflection or praxis, i.e. on what is possible, what is impossible.'[6]

This total critique of the totality, however, is not a collapse of dialectic back into the overcompensatory realms of wishful thinking. On the contrary, in emphasizing the end of one period of revolutionary praxis of the everyday, Lefebvre's revitalized commitment to the utopianism of Marx's programme is, at the same time, the passage of *truth through defeat*. This is a 'trilogy' that has absorbed both the dissolution of the radical energies of the postwar period of the Liberation, and the seemingly inexorable ossification of Stalinism in France and Eastern Europe. Thus culturally it owes far more to the neo-avant-garde's cultural ascendancy from 1960 than it does to the neo-realist programmes of the late 1940s and 1950s. The moment of realism in the production of the postwar category of the everyday – in identification with prewar documentary practices – is long gone.

The split in character of the 'trilogy', then, between disappointed hopes and replenished theoretical vigour, gives his extended critique of the everyday an unprecedented deflected or deflated character, putting his renewed commitment to Marx's programme under a quite different set of philosophical emphases than his work from the 1930s and *The Critique of Everyday Life, Vol. I.* The primordiality of becoming is stripped of all remnants of triumphalism, populism and false objectivism, to be represented under the deviant sign of irony. By this, Lefebvre does not mean that revolutionary praxis is in and of itself unbearingly hubristic, and therefore that it now needs irony to humanize it, but, rather, that history is itself an ironic, self-displacing process, insofar as human praxis is never completely transparent to itself. The primordiality of becoming is precisely the bringing forth of that which is least expected or wanted. Consequently the emergence of reason and truth is always immanent to error and untruth. 'There is a continual two-way dialectical movement between the true and the false, which transcends the historical situation that gave rise to these situations.'[7] This Hegelian defence of truth in error is given a coherent form in *Introduction to Modernity.*[8] Here Lefebvre develops a theory of Marxist irony or ironized Marxism under the self-ironizing gaze of Socrates.

Irony, Maieutics and the Everyday

What distinguishes the ironist, Lefebvre argues, is someone who risks the wrath of the powerful. In withdrawing consent from a given position, in taking a given truth to be partial or transient, the ironist is not afraid of setting himself or herself up as an agitator for truth. Irony, then, is a search for truth in protest against truth. This is why the protest for truth foresees its own failure, because, given that the ironist speaks from a defensive position, he or she cannot speak for the truth. The ironist insists on the possibility of truth, yet at the same time realizes he or she knows little or nothing. The ironist's sensitivity to the contingency of truth, then, brings dialectical thinking closer to the 'weak' thinking of Socratic dialogue. What Socrates does is not affirm or oppose a given proposition or assertion, he confronts it. 'The Socratic ironist does not choose between "knowing everything" and "knowing nothing". He knows something, and first and foremost that he knows nothing: therefore he knows what "knowing" is.'[9] This means that for Socrates irony and maieutic – the bringing forth of latent truths and ideas in 'weak thought' or illusion – cannot be separated. Indeed, one presupposes the other. So, irony does not stand in opposition to the universal claims of truth and dogmatism. Like dogmatism it represents a search for truth. But it is not the same kind of truth. It is a search for 'contingent or *possible* truth'.[10] For Lefebvre, Marxism today cannot live without this Socratic model. Or more precisely, it cannot live without Marx's own Socratic inclinations. Thus the ironic fire of Marxists must be directed not just against the bourgeoisie but against those who claim to be Marxists but who conspicuously fail the test of self-irony. Accordingly only Marxist irony can expose the becoming of Marxism. Thus to understand the significance of Marxist irony, the Marxist 'must understand the history of Marxism itself ironically, seeing it as a fragment of the prehistoric era of man'.[11]

Ironization, therefore, is not something that happens to revolutionary praxis once it is released from the demands of objectivity and truth. Rather, it is that which happens to revolutionary praxis once it is released from the dogmatism of the *unity* of theory and practice. Praxis and theory are not so much externally coherently related and mutually supportive, as internally divided and disjunctive. Hence, the ironist gains access to truth when he or she is objectively at their weakest: when theory fails to cohere with practice – that is, when theory exposes practice and practice exposes theory. For it is in the reflective gap between theory and practice – when theory and practice are internally and externally realigned – that the becoming of truth in its maieutic form emerges. Indeed, the Marxist ironist practises a kind of double maieutic: on theory *as* practice and practice *as* theory.

In this respect, Lefebvre subjects the universal identity of the proletariat to a thoroughly anti-Lukácsian ironization. The proletariat is not revolutionary by essence or structure. It is not a universal class by dint of its own idealized history or possible future identity, it is a revolutionary class, rather, in certain circumstances only and under certain conditions, circumstances and conditions which are not of its own choosing. Marx's privileging of the proletariat as the universal class, then, is true in as much as there is no universal class aside from the proletariat – the proletariat represents humanity in its totality of needs – but its universality as a revolutionary class is only ever conditional. This leads Lefebvre across the 'trilogy' to an extended defence of what had preoccupied him from his earliest writing on the philosophy of praxis: that in Marxism total revolutionary praxis is not a practice which knows itself transparently in accordance with its aims. The dialectic is not the theoretical expression of an already established and predictable historical structure, but the immanent critique of a structure which is transitive and open-ended. Thus if the ironization of history is on the one hand designed to decouple historical defeat from historical loss (defeat is not a loss to reason) it is, on the other hand, concerned to ground historical transformation in the aleatory and unpredictable event. 'If there is irony in history, it is because there is such a thing as history, real history with unforeseen tragedy and comedy. Conversely, because there really is history and the aleatory, there is such a thing as irony.'[12] In other words irony works 'both ways': it functions to displace defeat from irredeemable loss, and, at the same time, pays heed to the possibility of the radically new, the event which transforms the past and opens up the future. Marxist irony as the becoming of Marxism, therefore, is a kind of watchfulness over the contingent, in which 'chance [revolutionary action] expresses a necessity and expresses itself via a network of chances'.[13] In this way irony finds a cognate in risk, or the risk of the new, close in fact – ironically – to the early Lukács' notion of *Augenblick*: the idea that revolutionary action is of a necessity a leap into the unknown, given that there can never be an objective conjunction between revolutionary agency and a revolutionary situation.[14] Revolutionary action is always premature, so to speak. 'We must take into account the fact that every possibility contains risks, otherwise it would no longer be a possibility', declares Lefebvre.

Essentially, Lefebvre uses the notion of ironization to reformulate the notion of the 'irreducible remainder' in the critique of the everyday. The 'irreducible remainder' is not that which frees desire from reason, as in Schelling (or de Certeau), but that which opens up reason to its current historical limits. This is why the 'everyday' is never, for Lefebvre, reducible to its prevailing and historical forms; it is, rather, the place where desire attaches itself to the irreducible as reason. Hence Lefebvre makes a distinction between two operative forms of desire under the reign of the commodity and the colonization of everyday life: compulsive desire and adaptive desire. Compulsive desire is subject to the logic of accumulation, adaptive desire breaks with accumulation (intellectually as much as economically through the dynamic of capital) in order to open up the Moment to an awareness of the possible in the actual. These forms of desire, however, are in no sense separate; as in the everyday as such, inauthentic and authentic desire are continuous and interrelated, producing an 'incessant conflict between repression and evasion'.[15] But if adaption and compulsion are continuous and interrelated, compulsive desire is never able to contain adaptive desire, for the cathecting of desire with the 'irreducible' 'crops up again after each [compulsive] reduction'.[16] Desire in this sense is anomic:

'its social–extrasocial nature resists social and intellectual systematizations attempting to reduce it to a distinct, classified need satisfied as such'.[17] As a result, adaptive desire is the name increasingly given by Lefebvre in his writing after the Second World War to his notion of the critique of the everyday. In this sense, adaptive desire is what Marx's total revolutionary praxis encompasses, in so far as Marx's understanding of the term 'production' is – contrary to orthodoxy and Marx's legions of critics down to post-structuralism – not primarily economic. Indeed economistic philosophizing has obliterated the multi-accentuated content of the term in Marx's writing. For Marx, production

> signifies on the one hand 'spiritual' production, that is to say creations (including time and space) and on the other material production or the making of things; it also signifies the self-production of the 'human being' in the process of historical development.[18]

The defetishizing of productivity in political philosophy, of course, is the great counter-Marxian theme of critical theory and New Left post-Marxism in the 1960s and 1970s. But in contrast to Habermas, Lyotard, Foucault, Castoriados, de Certeau and others, Lefebvre does not place the critique of economism outside of the boundaries of Marx's programme for the revolutionary transformation of everyday life. Rather, he broadens its philosophical identity in keeping with what he believes to be Marx's identity between total revolutionary praxis and the transformation of everyday life. Hence an expanded account of production is key to Lefebvre's understanding of the critique of the everyday and its continuing possibilities, what he calls in *Everyday Life in the Modern World* 'Towards a Permanent Cultural Revolution'. The critique of everyday life is not directed towards creating an aesthetic transformation of prevailing social relations, in which producers become artists. Neither is it, he emphasizes, a revolution based simply on culture, in which social reality is mediated by newly minted revolutionary cultural institutions. Rather, cultural revolution is the transformation of the categories of experience itself. That is, culture (art, aesthetic experience) is directed towards the unpacking and dissolution of the alienated distinction between culture and everyday life. The revolutionary critique of the everyday, ultimately, is the production of a new 'life style' – of new forms of being and doing.

> From an intellectual point of view the word 'creation' will no longer be restricted to works of art but will signify a self-conscious activity, self-conceiving, reproducing its own terms, adapting these terms and its own reality (body, desire, time, space), being its own creation; socially the term will stand for the activity of a collectivity assuming the responsibility of its own social function and destiny – in other words for self-administration.[19]

Festivity Contra Technicity

This emancipatory horizon, of course, is what Lefebvre sees in the revolutionary incubus of the Situationist International, and as such defines that moment in the 1960s where the critique of the everyday brings Marx's total revolutionary praxis into explicit conflict with the legacy of Bolshevik machino-technism and other left-technocratic solutions to the problem of cultural form – although, strangely, Lefebvre not only sees the new cultural revolution as implicit in Lenin and Trotsky, but also nascent in Mao Tse-tung.[20] That Mao's cultural revolution was, despite its rhetoric, *utterly* technocratic in orientation – clearing out would-be pre-revolutionary and counter-revolutionary elements in order to hasten and improve the technological transformation of China – this is *egregiously* ironic on Lefebvre's part. But Maoism in France in the late 1960s was very much a pandemic on the left, so that Lefebvre no doubt felt obliged to show an affinity with it through his shift to a 'politics of desire'. Nevertheless, if this is embarrassing and unfathomable in the light of Lefebvre's commitment to total revolutionary praxis, it does point to a recurring set of problems around culture and technology and the technocratic that appear regularly in the later writing. As with the Situationists, Lefebvre's commitment to the revolutionary transformation of the everyday takes its measure critically from the value-form by keeping a distance from technological mediation. Repeatedly, Lefebvre identifies the critique of the everyday and the critique of the category of culture with the spontaneous bursting through of adaptive desire. This betrays the same indifference to *Technik* as in Debord's and Vaneigem's *Lebensphilosophic* tendencies. The revolutionary critique of the everyday is not directed towards the transformation of the relations between technology, creativity and labour, but towards their dispersal and disaggregation into forms of unmediated creativity, or festivity. 'The aim is not to let festivals die out or disappear beneath all that is prosaic in the world. It is to unite the Festival with everyday life.'[21]

Lefebvre, then, is as guilty as orthodox Marxists in producing a misformulation of the place of the aesthetic in Marx's critique of political economy. Marx's critique of the political economy is certainly compatible with the critique of technism; the emancipation of labour is at the same time an emancipation from the discipline of the value-form as an emancipation from the discipline of machines. This is key to *Capital*'s categories. But this liberation of sensuous form is not a liberation from technique, that is from the non-instrumental uses of technology. Indeed, the supersession of the value-form implies the liberation of non-instrumental use values from technology. Technology, then, also remains the place where creative use values will be adapted and developed *in* the revolutionary critique of everyday life. Too often, though, Lefebvre dismisses technology and technicity as things that prevent the spontaneity of the Moment and the unmediated relations of festivity from finding their expression. This has much to do with the fact that in the 'trilogy' Lefebvre fails to employ the category of labour in any consistent, dialectic sense. Labour is too often seen as the thing that is 'disappearing' under the colonization of the everyday. Moreover, intellectual labour in the form of the rise of metalanguage or, in post-1970s parlance, intertextuality, is repeatedly attacked for veiling or deflecting the authenticity of an experience or the reception of an artifact. This produces, particularly in *Everyday Life in the Modern World*, a contradiction between Lefebvre's commitment to Marx's identification between human emancipation and the theoretical development of the senses, and his defence of pre-metalanguage culture as an emancipation from the tyranny of the commodity form. In an eerie echo of late Lukács, Lefebvre loses sight of technical mediation as a way of refounding and developing the senses and of cultural practice. The concept of the festivity, then, is thoroughly undertheorized. It may link everyday life with the possibility of unmediated pleasures, but the release of social singularities through these pleasures is no guarantee of liberation. Indeed, the opposite might apply: festivity becomes the tyranny of the spontaneous particular in some hideous compulsion to enjoy.

In this light, in Lefebvre the overriding images of emancipation from labour are derived from primitive communism and the pastoral village community. Across his work from the 1930s to the 1960s he returns again and again to the identification of the emancipation of labour from the commodity form with the release of immediate and natural forms of necessity (cyclical time scales and forms of affective spontaneity). These ancient and cosmic cyclical scales and forms may have been largely been destroyed as cultural systems by capitalism and modernity, yet they have not become antediluvian remainders or disappeared completely. On the contrary, they survive in displaced and mediated practices and forms: in some modern agriculture, in language, in architecture, in music and dance, and painting. The periodicities and repetitions of these practices and forms, therefore, may be subject to the disciplinarity of the commodity form – to its calendrical order – but they do not derive from its logic. 'The spontaneous is already part of

the social, although it is not the social per se.'[22] Moreover, for
Lefebvre these cycles and affective forms also survive in aspects
of the 'feminine' and the cultural and physiological experience
of women. From ancient cultures to the present, he suggests,
women have been the custodians of various non-linear forms,
symbols and practices.

> How prosaic and tedious these norms and representations are,
> but also how tenacious in praxis, and how profound: everything
> involving the house, the 'home' and domesticity, and thus everyday
> life. At the same time, both symbolically and as conscious 'subjects'
> they embody the loftiest values of art, ethics and culture: love,
> passions and virtues, beauty, nobility, sacrifice, permanence.[23]

This anthropologization of the feminine is certainly not the
most suasive part of his defence of non-linearity and 'non-
capitalist' time here. By the 1960s the increased entry of women
into the workforce made claims for the symbolic continuity of
women and 'home' risible. Similar the lofty identification of
women with the arts appears to have been borrowed from the
conservative organicism of the 1880s. But it certainly makes
clear what the relationship between adaptive desire and total
praxis had come to mean for Lefebvre by the mid-1960s: a
critique of the everyday as a critique of the tripartite structure
of the time of accumulation: pledged time (labour time), free
time (leisure) and compulsive time (transportation to work and
related work and family duties). For Lefebvre, then, any kind
of residual forms or practices that might stand in asymmetrical
relation to the linear and technical logic of accumulation – from
the 'feminine' to the negations of the neo-avant-garde – are
brought in under the mantle of total revolutionary praxis and
the critique of the everyday. This is why by the early 1960s
Lefebvre's defence of the possible in the actual is itself not
immune to the attractions of a nascent micro-politics opened
up by the Situationists, in contrastinction to official working-
class politics. In *Introduction to Modernity*, in direct dialogue
with the group, he synthesizes his theory of the Moment and

his version of the irreducible remainder into a theory of the revolutionary groupuscle. For Lefebvre, what is particularly incisive about the Situationists is that as a disciplined unit they explore and test out various forms of non-accumulative practice as a *lived* utopianism. In disregarding the pieties of labour, official art and culture, their praxis of negation opens up the actual into the 'possible–impossible' dialectic, paving the way for a new lifestyle; as such their programme 'brings together in a single ensemble the working-class struggle in all its forms and on all its levels'.[24]

This brings us back to the tripartite split I noted in Benjamin's writing in Chapter 1 between the critique of the everyday as the reified 'reproduction of the immediate' (Lukács); the critique of the everyday as the utopian dissolution of art into the everyday (Constructivism and Productivism); and the critique of the everyday as the representation *of* the everyday (the rehistoricization of everyday life). Following the Situationists, Lefebvre abrogates the latter in favour of the first position as mediated through an aestheticized anti-technist reading of the second position. This leaves his defence of the critique of the everyday as a defence of Marx's total revolutionary praxis in a space which is some distance from the anti-technist *Technik* of the early Soviet avant-garde – initially his other great intellectual mentor. How can festivity secure and develop the creativity of the intellect as sensuous practice? How can festivity provide the conditions for individual self-realization?

Marx's conception of self-realization in the 'Economic and Philosophic Manuscripts' is based on the Enlightenment German tradition of *Bildung*.[25] Cultural self-realization comes not through adherence to the replication and reproduction of inherited models of cultural practice, or through the release of spontaneous feelings, but through self-developing communities of intellect. Self-realization lies, therefore, in the development of cognitive and creative spaces for reflection and self-reflection, what Marx calls 'the rich, living, sensuous concrete activity of self-objectification'.[26] And, of necessity, these spaces will be governed by practices of mutual and (self-critical) learning. Consequently within the tradition of *Bildung*, culture and intellectual labour (and labour *on* the self) are not opposed. Cultural development is derived precisely from those forms of objectification provided by intellectual labour. This means that authentic cultural self-realization lies in the expansion of the scope of aesthetic reason and not in the encouragement of aesthetic desublimation. Accordingly, we might talk, as we have done in relation to the Situationists, about the premature dissolution of the cultural tasks of representation and the abstract concept under Lefebvre's theory of the Moment and notion of festivity. As such, we might ask, where precisely is the sensuous–practical content of Marx's total revolutionary practice in Lefebvre's account?

Lefebvre is right to insist that Marx's revolutionary programme has two major and interrelated components: the aesthetic and the ethical. And that the critique of political economy – in *Capital* – implicitly underwrites these two components' explicit manifestation in the philosophical early writings. He is also right to criticize Marx for his occasional tendency to subordinate the process of world-historical becoming to art, rather than art to world-historical becoming.[27] Art will not escape the dissolution of the distinction between everyday practice and social technique. This is the great emancipatory theme of the critique of the everyday from Arvatov onwards, underwriting the expansion of aesthetic reason. But, because both Lefebvre and the Situationists have little use for or faith in the concept of art beyond the rhetoric of neo-avant-garde intervention, the position of cultural practice in the here and now becomes highly attenuated. In fact, ironically, there is an unnerving overlap between their dismissal of contemporary art, and orthodox Marxism's espousal in the 1940s and 1950s of the decadence of modern art. This is not to say that Lefebvre does not have some sympathy for some neo-avant-garde practices, but he is not interested in how neo-avant-garde practice might secure some of the things he imagines Marx's total revolutionary praxis might secure.

This is why we need to return to a discussion of praxis, and in particular Lukács and Benjamin, in order to clarify the relationship between the total critique of everyday life, art and cultural practice.

Praxis – Technik – Bildung

What is of central importance to Lukács' critique of reification is that it is forged out of a Hegelian insistence on theoretical self-consciousness as an inherently *practical* and sensuous matter. Theoretical practice has material and transformative effects on practice, and therefore material and transformative effects in the world. This is why the concept of the everyday achieves its initial critical dynamism in the 1920s precisely through the philosophy of praxis's critique of the non-dialectical categories of prewar German sociology and the reflection theory of orthodox Marxism. The job of Marxism is not to oppose 'true appearances' to 'false appearances', but to insist on practice as form of knowledge and therefore theoretical knowledge as a part *of* social reality.[28] This is why the Hegelian notion of situated knowledge and agency plays such a determining role in the theorization of the everyday from the Russian Revolution through to Benjamin and Lefebvre and the Situationists. The situation (or, more broadly, the concrete conjuncture) is the finite and localizable place where sensuous–theoretical activity is embedded, that is, the place where the everyday is constituted, challenged, reproduced, materially and historically.

The emergence of the concept of the everyday in Lukács' and Benjamin's writing, is based precisely, therefore, on defining intellectual labour and cultural activity as forms of sensuous–material praxis. This, in turn, means that explicit in their writing is the need to transform our understanding of the relationship between the technical and material base of culture and the technical and material base of the relations of production. Cultural practices, technology and technicity are *not* opposed, but are the interrelated means by which the everyday is to be transformed and restructured 'from the base' upwards. Culture is not an inert space of aesthetic traditions and technologies, but a means of their mutual transformation. Culture is a constellation of sensuous–theoretical activities through which the shared self-consciousness of the producer and consumer (as producer) stand in a practical and transformative relation to the world. As Lukács was to argue in 1918: 'politics is merely a means, culture is the goal'[29] – that is, the creation of genuine and autonomous human culture is to be forged from the destruction of the reified social relations and objectified technological practices of capitalist society. Thus, the enculturalization of the everyday in the early Lukács and Benjamin operates under two related claims: (1) as a critique of the economic determinism of orthodox Marxism on matters of cultural agency and interpretation; and (2) as a critique of the bourgeois separation of cultural form *from* the relations of production.

Lukács and Benjamin initially share this vision of culture.[30] But, unlike Lukács, Benjamin takes this in an explicitly politicized avant-garde direction, and for good reason: it is only through the *advanced* cultural adaptation of technological and technical relations that sensuous–theoretical activity is able to achieve these practical conditions of shared critical self-consciousness, allowing the proletariat to take their democratic place within modern culture, and allowing for the universal conditions of self-transformation to emerge. Hence the primary *cultural* significance of the technism/anti-technism debate of the Russian Revolution for Benjamin, and for our discussion of the everyday. As an emancipatory force, culture is not just the place where people find pleasure or attain knowledge in the abstract, or a place of future unmediated festivity or

aesthetic desublimation, but an experimental training ground
in new kinds of interaction and sociability between technology,
cognition and cultural form.[31]

In this respect Benjamin is one of the few major theorists
of culture and the everyday for whom the form of cultural
production is integral to a discussion of technology and
technicity. This is because such interrelations between
technology and technicity on the terrain of cultural practice
were for Benjamin constitutive of the emancipatory possibilities
of the philosophy of praxis. As we have seen, Lefebvre follows
Benjamin in defending the notion of cultural practice as socially
transformative practice. But after the Second World War there
is less interest in his writing in the revolutionary conditions
of the technical transformation of the relations of cultural
production than in the formation and channelling of cultural
praxis as a kind of revolutionary *elan*, or aestheticization of
social practice as revolutionary 'lifestyle'. This is because by
the 1950s and 1960s, a defence of the dialectical unity of
theory and practice as cultural praxis – what we might call
the founding thesis of the philosophy of praxis – was in an
impossibly weakened position politically – as Lefebvre was
fully aware in his writing in the late 1950s. Twenty-five years
of Stalinism and a buoyant social democracy had made the
socially and culturally transformative content of the philosophy
of praxis an empty and academic ideal. The residual non-
bourgeois content in Benjamin's Productivist model had been
overtaken by the culture industry; whatever new social relations
had been developed between art, technology and technicity
had been colonized by the art world.

This undoubtedly had an effect on the development of
the promissory category of the festival in Lefebvre and the
Situationists, over and above a defence of the prospects of
revolutionary *Technik*. Thus, instead of developing a post-
Benjaminan Adornian line on art through insisting on
neo-avant-garde forms and practices as one of the remaining

primary promissory spaces of cultural self-realization (a revolutionary hermeneutics, so to speak), Lefebvre and the Situationists identified cultural liberation and the possibility of self-realization outside of the confines of art as intellectual labour. This left them with a one-dimensional account of *Bildung*, reflected in their exaggerated recourse to a philosophy of individual self-action, Vaneigem being the worst offender. The immediate results of this negation in the 1950s might have appeared productive in an emerging world of technocratic reason, but eventually it produced the very reversal of the Situationists' actual revolutionary intentions: the reinvention of the everyday into new forms of self-aestheticizing counter-cultural gesturalism. By traducing the space of intellectual labour in art, the emancipatory promise of anti-art fell into a kind of bloated anti-bourgeois and anti-Stalinist rhetoric. The counter-cultural explosion of May 1968, of course, didn't transform these prospects to any great extent. After the proto-revolution's defeat, the defence of the post-art gesture as the promise of total revolutionary praxis merely redoubled the sense of the long-term stasis immanent to the concept of festivity. As such, the real and genuine destabilizing energies of 1968 easily passed into the long depolitical thaw and downturn in class struggle of the 1980s and 1990s and as such into various forms of cultural nihilism or bland affirmation of multiculturalism.[32]

In this light, in the absence of the conditions for the total revolutionary critique of the everyday, from the 1970s the everyday has been required to do a huge amount of critically transformative work. And this is why Lefebvre and the Situationists tended to despise the critical claims of neo-avant-garde practice, and why the Situationists ended up despising Lefebvre so much, because of Lefebvre's willingness to give in occasionally to this tendency: the fact that the critique of the everyday had become consanguineous with a culturally approved critique of the everyday. But, to put it another way, the radicalization of culture since the 1960s has been successful precisely *because* of its compensatory and deflected nature. Or to put it in yet another register, the displacement of total revolutionary praxis by the cultural hermeneutic model of the everyday from the 1930s onwards is necessarily double-coded. Under the rise of cultural studies and the return to Simmel-like defences of the 'creative consumer', the analysis of cultural form and capitalism has been suppressed or sidelined. Cultural studies has generally made peace with the alienations of labour and the revolutionary power of *Bildung*. However, the rise of the hermeneutic model has also allowed cultural theory to free the popular spectator and consumer from the travails of reification theory, and therefore to expose Western Marxism's own weaknesses (in particular the concept of 'instrumental reason' and its condescension towards popular culture). Thus, at the point of the demise of the concept of total revolutionary praxis, it is the hermeneutic model of the everyday that is one of the very means of holding onto its revolutionary memory. For it is through work *on* the representation of the everyday, that is, through the rehistoricization of the everyday, that the critique of the everyday is able to be reproduced and sustained as cultural practice. In this respect, despite his model of ironized reflection, Lefebvre's emphasis on the deadening rise of the effects of metalanguage on creativity, and the colonization of art as aesthetics, drives a wedge between cultural practice and the sign as the home of the utopian unconscious, diminishing the possibilities for this process of rehistoricization. And if this is precisely the point where we entered the debate on the everyday in the 1930s with Benjamin, it is precisely where we must now leave it.

Epilogue

It is possible to discern a fundamental transformation of the democratic content of the concept of the everyday in the twentieth century. Under its revolutionary emergence in the early 1920s the demotic identity of the concept was integral *to* the demands and expectations of revolutionary change and proletarian agency. The arrival to power of a subaltern consciousness of the everyday into the experience of a shared, common culture was to enact the promise of the total dehierarchization and dealienation of capitalist production and social relations. In short, to identify and defend the concept of the everyday was to see it as a space where praxis and reason were united. Hence the importance of Productivism and Constructivism in the 1920s and 1930s in the early formation of the concept.

In the post-Bolshevik period of the early development of cultural studies in postwar France, the memory of this revolutionary elision between praxis and reason was transformed into a process of cultural democratization internal to the new conditions of mass culture. In this, the everyday became the signifier of socialist democratization *through* cultural change. To defend the everyday as the space of democratic transformation was to give value to those things and experiences 'from below' that state modernization, bourgeois high culture and the abstractions of the market occluded – hence the increasing identification between the everyday and the notion of the symbolic remainder, and, in the widest sense, the importance of the aesthetics of montage. In the third – post-Situationist – period, this fledgling connection between the everyday and the symbolic others of capitalist repression and modernist abstraction became a systematic theory of the non-identitary and of multiple subjectivity. To identify, defend and critique the everyday is in effect to seek and reclaim the culturally and socially marginal and the cultural autonomy of the subaltern subject; the everyday is the site of the 'voiceless'.

From this point an unprecedented reversal overtakes the content of the everyday: at the same time as the conditions of monopolization deepen the uniformity of daily experience across capitalist culture, in the new cultural theory the everyday as the site of the irreducible symbolic remainder becomes a hugely expanded site of interpretative freedom, cultural activity and popular pleasures. Mass culture not only becomes a site of contestation through its non-passive consumption, but the production of popular counter-cultures become sites of would-be political resistance, education and autonomy. But what this produces, paradoxically, is the increasing dissolution of the revolutionary content of the everyday as a signifier of cultural democracy itself. Under the simultaneous expansion of the meanings of culture and the critical demassification of mass culture, the critique of the everyday is assimilated to the pleasures of capitalist everydayness. That is, the expanded individuation, dissemination, and reproduction of the meanings of the dominated as popular pleasures is incorporated into a new consumerist counter-culture.

But if this strengthens the necessary link between the democratization of representation and collective struggle 'from below', it also weakens the links between democratization and cultural production, hermeneutics and revolutionary praxis. De Certeau's *The Practice of Everyday Life* is indicative in this respect, in so far as it contributes to the postmodern incorporation of the redefinition of the everyday as a site of complex and differentiated social agency and subjectivity into the 'politics of representation' separate from any structural engagement with the problems of material distribution and economic justice.[1]

Hence, if moments of autonomy and signs of dissent can be discerned in all forms of mass culture, and popular cultures function as sites of creative resistance, the dehierarchizing function of the everyday loses its former negative political leverage. The notion of the 'irreducible remainder', in fact, no longer signifies the utopian trace or space for practices of another *rationality* – as in Arvatov, Benjamin, Lefebvre and the Situationists – but a confirmation of the powers of the creative consumer and the superior democracy of community politics. The contemporary ecumenical force of the concept as a post-ideological version of the 'creative consumer' is now identifiable with this apparent triumph of the redemptive or open model of ideology in cultural studies. In this way, the democratic content of the everyday has become overly identified with the celebration of popular *representations* at the expense of the categories of praxis, *Technik* and *Bildung*.

The dehistoricization of the everyday, then, follows the general depoliticizing thrust of contemporary cultural studies in the 1990s. The everyday has become so enmeshed in an affirmative anthropological model of subaltern subject positions, that it has become convergent with the institutions, spaces and social relations of the advanced capitalist consumer economy. Social and cultural division are left behind as a kind of hindrance to the identification and production of the 'local' and 'particularistic'. Indeed, the relations between the everyday and 'hegemony' no longer refer to the power of ruling classes to conceal and promote their interests through forms of popular consent, but to an affirmation of subaltern politics in a struggle against 'corporate ideology'. Whereas forms of popular agency once 'liberated' the everyday from ideology, they now dissolve ideology into the everyday. Consequently, after three decades of cultural studies the concept of the everyday is now also the site of the active repression of its own post-capitalist and avant-garde 'anti-art' history. Which means that if the new differentiated social subject expands the content of the everyday, it has done so at the expense of the everyday's historical and critical relationship to its *non-contemporaneous* temporalities. As Arvatov, Lefebvre and the Situationists understood, the critique of the everyday is also driven by the *promise of the everyday's own demise.*

This is why, for all the concept's contemporary dehistoricization, the tropological content of the 'everyday' continues to possess extraordinary powers of invocation. When one tries to imagine a genealogy of synonyms of the concept, such as the 'ordinary' or the 'daily', they simply don't possess the same depth and powers of abstraction. In short, they remain conceptually and historically inert. This is because the critique of the everyday is not just a form of anthropological or ethnographical reading, but, rather, a utopian and historically discontinuous space through which struggles over the cultural form of art, technology, technique and aesthetic experience and *Bildung* are fought out. This is why, despite the everyday's absorption into a philosophically diminished cultural studies, it is necessary that we derive the critical meanings of the concept from the constellation of competing political temporalities and spatialities from which it has emerged. In this, hermeneutics continues to reflect on, and awaken, the promissory space of total revolutionary praxis.

Notes

Prologue: Dangerous Memories

1. For example, Hugh MacKay (ed.), *Consumption and Everyday Life* (London: Sage Publications, in association with the Open University, 1997); Brian Massumi (ed.), *The Politics of Everyday Fear* (Mineapolis: University of Minnesota Press, 1993); 'The Epic and the Everyday: Contemporary Photographic Art' (South Bank Gallery, London, 1994); 'Everyday', 11th Biennale of Sydney (Art Gallery of New South Wales, 1998).

2. Similarly, in analytical philosophy the semantic and cognitive pinning down of 'ordinariness' (in language use) and the pursuit of 'ordinary' (unaffected, plain, discreet) conceptions of the common good have determined much post-metaphysical ethics and philosophy of language.

3. See David Chaney, *Cultural Change and Everyday Life* (London: Palgrave, 2002). Similarly Ben Highmore in *Everyday Life and Cultural Theory: An Introduction* (London and New York: Routledge, 2002) declares in a de Certeauian register, that rescuing 'the traces, the remainders of the overflowing unmanageability of the everyday' (p. 26) allows us to propose and recover an everyday of the *improper*. Admittedly Highmore is no simple-minded defender of the resistant within the dominant, but his work fits comfortably into a wider pattern of accommodation to the everyday as a representational and archival category. That is, what is interesting about the everyday is precisely our worldly immersion in our failure to apprehend it.

4. For an excellent critique of contemporary cultural studies in these terms, see John Kraniauskas, 'Globalization is Ordinary', *Radical Philosophy*, No. 90, July/August 1998.

5. However, with the emergence of the concept of the 'everyday' in the new cultural studies, art theory and urban studies since the early 1990s, Lefebvre's writing in Britain and North America has undergone a renaissance in readership.

6. Stanley Aronowitz, *Roll Over Beethoven: The Return of Cultural Studies* (Wesleyan University Press, 1993).

7. John Roberts, *The Art of Interruption: Realism, Photography and the Everyday* (Manchester: Manchester University Press, 1998).

8. For a discussion of this fragile alliance, see Sam Rohdie, *The Passion of Pier Paolo Pasolini* (London and Bloomington: British Film Institute/Indiana University Press, 1995).

9. For a recent discussion of the cultural and political dynamics of May 1968, see Kristin Ross, *May '68 and its Afterlives* (Chicago and London: University of Chicago Press, 2002). One would also want to include in this short period of modernist counter-cultural ascendancy the fertile meeting between the far left (Cacciari, Tronti, Negri) and revolutionary cultural theorists in Italy in the late 1960s, in particular the work of Manfredo Tafuri (see *Architecture and Utopia: Design and Capitalist Development* (Cambridge, Massachusetts and London: MIT Press, 1992); but in contrast to Lefebvre and the Situationists, there is little discussion of the everyday in this writing. For present purposes, then, it is better left out of my narrative.

10. Henri Lefebvre puts the loss of this counter-hegemony earlier. The bourgeoisie 'possibly lost [the quotidian, the everyday] between the years 1917 and 1933; but from 1950 on the situation was reversed'. However, he did write this a couple of years before May 1968. See *Everyday Life in the Modern World*, translated by Sacha Rabinovitch, with a new introduction by Philip Wander (London: Athlone Press, 2000), p. 41.

11. Henri Lefebvre, *The Critique of Everyday Life, Vol. II: Foundations for a Sociology of the Everyday*, translated by John Moore, with a preface by Michel Trebitsch (London and New York: Verso, 2002), p. 93.

12. This is the problem with Perry Anderson's *Considerations on Western Marxism* (London: New Left Books, 1976), which could be said to actually reverse the critical achievements of this epoch. For Anderson, Western Marxism fails conspicuously because of its culturalism, and, as such, its retreat from classical forms of political praxis. However, it is the opposite that might be said to apply in this period: Western Marxism is at its most interesting precisely when it *is* culturalist, that is, when it opens up orthodox Marxism and its classical legacy to a critique of its incipient technism and the Bolshevik love of Taylorism (Benjamin, early Lukács, Korsch and some parts of Gramsci). Without this cultural opening up of praxis, there can in fact be no collective and emancipatory praxis worthy of the name.

13. I borrow the concept 'dangerous memory' from Johann Baptist Metz. See 'Prophetic Authority' in Jürgen Moltmann, Herbert W. Richardson, Johann Baptist Metz, Willi Oelmüller and M. Darrol

Bryant, *Religion and Political Society* (London and New York: Harper & Row, 1974).

14. Lefevbre, *The Critique of Everyday Life, Vol. II*, p. 37.
15. Karl Marx, *Grundrisse* (Harmondsworth: Penguin, 1973), p. 100.
16. For example, the work of Kristin Ross. See her 'French Quotidian', in Lynn Gumpert (ed.), *The Art of the Everyday: The Quotidian in Postwar French Culture* (New York: New York University Press, 1997); and *Fast Cars, Clean Bodies: Decolonization and The Reordering of French Culture* (Cambridge, Massachusetts and London: MIT Press, 1995).

1 The Everyday and the Philosophy of Praxis

1. Karl Marx, *A Contribution to the Critique of Political Economy*, translated by N. I. Stone (Chicago: Charles H. Kerr Publishing, 1904), p. 30.
2. See Georg Lukács, *Theory of the Novel* (London: Merlin Press, 1971).
3. For a discussion of *Lebensphilosophie* and pre-First World War European culture, see György Márkus, 'Life and the Soul: the Young Lukács and the Problem of Culture', in Agnes Heller (ed.) *Lukács Revalued* (Oxford: Basil Blackwell, 1983).
4. Martin Heidegger, *Being and Time* (Oxford: Basil Blackwell, 1962).
5. See, Georg Lukács, *Tactics and Ethics: Political Writings, 1919–1929* (London: New Left Books, 1972).
6. Georg Lukács, *Soul and Form*, translated by Anna Bostock (Cambridge, Massachusetts: MIT Press, 1971 [1910]), p. 233.
7. Sigmund Freud, *The Psychopathology of Everyday Life* (London and Glasgow: Collins, 1958), p. 11.
8. The high-point of this debate in the Soviet Union was V. N. Volishinov's *Freudianism: A Marxist Critique*, translated by I. R. Titunik and edited in collaboration with Neal H. Bruss (New York, 1976).
9. Freud's *The Interpretation of Dreams* was published in 1900, *The Psychopathology of Everyday Life* in 1901. As Freud was to say in 1890 in 'psychical' (or mental) treatment, '[w]ords are the essential tool of mental treatment ... for the words which we use in our everyday speech are nothing other than watered-down magic'. *The Standard Edition of the Complete Psychological Works*, 24 vols, Vol. 11 (London: Hogarth Press and the Institute of Psychoanalysis, 1953–74), p. 283.

10. Leon Trotsky, *Problems of Everyday Life, and Other Writings on Culture and Science* (New York: Pathfinder Press, 1973).

11. Leon Trotsky, 'How to Begin', in *Problems*, p. 70.

12. Leon Trotsky, 'Leninism and Library Work', in *Problems*, p. 143.

13. Leon Trotsky, 'The Struggle for Cultural Speech', in *Problems*, p. 59.

14. Ibid., p. 60.

15. Alexandra Kollantai, 'Marriage and Everyday Life', in *Alexandra Kollantai: Selected Writings*, translated and with commentaries by Alix Holt (London: Allison & Busby, 1977). See also *Love of Worker Bees*, with an introduction by Cathy Porter and an afterword by Sheila Rowbotham (London: Virago, 1977); and *The Autobiography of a Sexually Emancipated Communist Woman*, translated by Salvator Attensio (New York: Herder & Herder, 1971). On femininity, the feminine and the everyday see Henri Lefebvre, *Critique de la vie quotidienne II: Fondements d'une sociologie de la quotidienneté* (Paris: L'Arche Editeur, 1961), translated as *The Critique of Everyday Life, Vol. II: Foundations for a Sociology of the Everyday*.

16. Leon Trotsky, 'Introduction to the Tatar-language Edition', in *Problems*, p. 79.

17. Alexandra Kollantai, *Red Love* (New York: Seven Arts Publishing Co., 1927 [1923]).

18. V. I. Lenin, 'Immediate Tasks of the Soviet Government', in *Collected Works*, Vol. 27 (Moscow: Progress Publishers, 1972).

19. Trotsky, *Problems*, p. 243.

20. Alexei Gastev, quoted in René Fülöp-Miller, *The Mind and Face of Bolshevism: An Examination of Cultural Life in Soviet Russia*, translated by F. S. Flint and D. F. Tait (London and New York: G. P. Putnam's Sons, 1927), p. 207. For a discussion of Gastev and the rationalization of labour, see also Thomas F. Remington, *Building Socialism in Bolshevik Russia: Ideology and Industrial Organization 1917–1921* (Pittsburgh and London: University of Pittsburgh Press, 1984).

21. Alexei Gastev, in Fülop-Miller, *Bolshevism*, p. 210.

22. See Victor Margolin, *The Struggle For Utopia: Rodchenko, Lissitzky, Moholy-nagy 1917–1946* (Chicago: University of Chicago Press, 1997). See also John E. Bowlt, 'Manipulating Metaphors: El Lissitzky and the Crafted Hand', in Nancy Perloff and Brian Reed (eds), *Situating El Lissitzky: Vitebsk, Berlin, Moscow* (Los Angeles: Getty Research Institute, 2003).

23. Leon Trotsky, *History of the Russian Revolution* (New York: Pathfinder Press, 1980).

24. Victor Serge, *Year One of the Russian Revolution*, translated and edited by Peter Sedgwick with a new preface by Paul Foot (London

and New York: Bookmarks/Pluto Press/Writers and Readers, 1992).
First published as *L'An 1 de la révolution russe* (Paris, 1930).

25. Ante Ciliga, *The Russian Enigma*, part one translated by Fernand
    G. Fernier and Anne Cliff, part two translated by Margaret and
    Hugo Dewar (London: Ink Links, 1979). First published as *Au pays
    du grand mensonage* [*In the Land of the Great Lie*] (Paris, 1938).
26. Fülöp-Miller, *Bolshevism*, p. 15.
27. Ibid., p. 24.
28. See Georg Plekhanov, *The Materialist Conception of History*
    (London: Lawrence & Wishart, 1976) and Karl Kautsky, *The
    Dictatorship of the Proletariat* (Ann Arbor: Michigan University
    Press, 1964).
29. See John Roberts, *The Art of Interruption: Realism, Photography
    and the Everyday* (Manchester: Manchester University Press,
    1998).
30. Karl Marx, 'Theses on Feuerbach', in Karl Marx and Frederick
    Engels, *Collected Works*, Vol. 5 (London: Lawrence & Wishart,
    1976). For a defence and overview of the philosophy of praxis
    – although without reference to the everyday – see Adolfo Sánchez
    Vásquez, *The Philosophy of Praxis*, translated by Mike Gonzalez
    (London and New Jersey: Merlin Press/Humanities Press, 1977).
31. Karl Korsch, *Marxism and Philosophy* (London: New Left Books,
    1970).
32. Georg Lukács, *History and Class Consciousness: Studies in Marxist
    Dialectics* (London: Merlin, 1971).
33. Georg Lukács, *Lenin: A Study on the Unity of His Thought* (London:
    New Left Books, 1970).
34. Ibid., p. 13. As Lukács was also to affirm 50 years later, ' whatever
    you are doing, as a scientist or anything else, you always start from
    the problems of everyday life' (p. 13); 'if I start from the categorical
    imperative, I will not be able to understand the simple practical
    behaviour of people in everyday life' (p. 15). *Conversations with
    Lukács*, edited by Theo Pinkus (London: Merlin, 1974).
35. Lukács, *History and Class Consciousness*, p. xliii.
36. Lukács, *Lenin*, p. 92.
37. Korsch, *Marxism and Philosophy*, p. 54.
38. Ibid., p. 64.
39. Ibid., p. 71.
40. Ibid., p. 78.
41. 'The Present State of the Problem of Marxism and Philosophy: An
    Anti-Critique' (1930), in Korsch, *Marxism and Philosophy*.
42. Frederick Engels, *Ludwig Feuerbach and the End of Classical
    Philosophy* (Peking: Foreign Language Press, 1976), p. 60.
43. Korsch, *Marxism and Philosophy*, p. 82.

44. Lukács, *History and Class Consciousness*, p. 197.
45. Ibid., pp. 15–16. The wider philosophical significance of *History and Class Consciousness* lies in its critical extension of Hegel's and Marx's 'solution' to the idealist antinomy of the particular and the universal. With the development of Hegel's and Marx's understanding of historically developing social consciousness, particularity could no longer be seen as the negation of universality but as its embodiment. Universality is now no longer *opposed to the everyday, but is immanent to it*. Hence, under the collective self-knowledge of the proletariat, critical praxis actively 'restructur[es] the real' (p. 193). In this 'we shall have raised ourselves ... to the position from which reality can be understood as our action' (p. 145).
46. Ibid., p. 39.
47. Ibid., p. 76.
48. Karl Korsch, 'The Present State of the Problem of Marxism and Philosophy: An Anti-Critique' (1930), in *Marxism and Philosophy*, p. 106.
49. Lukács, *History and Class Consciousness*, p. xviii.
50. Henri Lefebvre, 'Foreword to the fifth edition', *Dialectical Materialism* (London: Jonathan Cape, 1968), p. 17.
51. Henri Lefebvre, *Sociologie de Marx* (Paris: Presse Universitaires de France, 1966); translated as *The Sociology of Marx* (Harmondsworth: Allen Lane, Penguin Press, 1968), p. 36.
52. Lefebvre, *Dialectical Materialism*, p. 100.
53. Ibid., p. 102.
54. Ibid., p. 70.
55. Ibid., p. 128.
56. Antonio Gramsci, *Selections from Prison Notebooks*, edited and translated by Quintin Hoare and Geoffrey Nowell Smith (London: Lawrence & Wishart, 1971), p. 331.
57. Ibid., p. 326.
58. Ibid., p. 377.
59. Ibid., p. 421.
60. Ibid., p. 424.
61. Ibid., p. 417.
62. Lefebvre, *Dialectical Materialism*, p. 96.
63. Georg Simmel, *Philosophie des Geldes* (Duncker & Humblot, 1907); English translation, *The Philosophy of Money*, translated by Tom Bottomore and David Frisby (Routledge & Kegan Paul, London, 1978).
64. Lukács, *History and Class Consciousness*, pp. 156–7.
65. Martin Heidegger, *Being and Time* (Oxford: Basil Blackwell, 1962), pp. 138–48.

66. Ibid., pp. 163–8. In Heidegger the 'everyday', as a world of
    technological becoming or unfolding, is inauthentic precisely because
    the revealing, or Enframing, of human activity and consciousness it
    puts in place – the objectifications and taxonomies of science – allows
    nothing to be experienced as it is 'in itself', at hand, spontaneously.
    The everyday thus blocks the summons of Being, the submitting to
    the openness-to-Being. But it is in the concealment of the everyday
    as the realm of revealing, or Enframing, that the unconcealment of
    the truth of Being – of Being brought into its own – will emerge in
    a 'flashing'. In this sense technology is not to be transcended, but
    restored to its essence, through the unfolding of technology as the
    concealment/unconcealment of Being. See Heidegger, *The Question
    Concerning Technology and Other Essays*, translated and with an
    introduction by William Lovitt (London and New York: Harper &
    Row, 1977).

67. Heidegger, *Being and Time*, p. 140.

68. Walter Benjamin, *Aufsätze, Essays, Vorträge: Gesammelte Schriften
    Band 2.3* (Frankfurt am Main: Suhrkamp, 1977), p. 1138.

69. Walter Benjamin, 'A Short History of Photography', *One Way Street*
    (London and New York: New Left Books), p. 251.

70. In the 'Artwork' essay there is a stronger sense of the 'everyday'
    as politically charged and conceptually distinct from the 'daily'.
    In the original German it reads: 'der Alltag illustrativ zubegleiten'
    ('to accompany the everyday illustratively') ('Das Kunstwerk im
    Zeitalter seiner technischen Reproduzuerbarkeit' (Dritte Fassung),
    p. 474). In the English translation in *Illuminations* (London:
    Fontana, 1973, p. 213) it reads: 'to illustrate everyday life'. The
    difference is important, because 'der Alltag' is a colloquialism for
    the 'daily grind', the 'everyday' is 'werktag' (work-day). In this
    sense 'der Alltag' is class inflected, insofar as it connotes everyday
    labour. So the difference is not just between 'täglichen lebens' and
    'Alltag lebens' but between 'Alltag lebens' and 'der Alltag'.

71. Walter Benjamin, 'In der UdSSR die Kunst in der Industrie und
    des Alltags lebens tritt', *Nachträge: Gesammelte Schirften, Band
    2.2* (Frankfurt am Main: Suhrkamp, 1989, p. 886). Another
    source of reference to the 'everyday' in Benjamin is to be found
    in his review of Siegfried Kracauer's *Die Angestellen* (1930), '"Ein
    Aussenseiter Macht Sich Bemerkbar" Zu S. Kracauer', in Walter
    Benjamin, *Kritiken under Rezensionen: Gesemmalte Schriften Band
    3* (Frankfurt am Main: Suhrhamp, 1991). This was translated as
    '"An Outsider Attracts Attention", on The Salaried Masses by S.
    Kracauer', in Siegfried Kracauer, *The Salaried Masses: Duty and
    Distraction in Weimar Germany*, translated by Quintin Hoare and
    introduced by Inka Mülder-Bach (London and New York: Verso,
    1998). 'There is no class today whose feeling is more alienated

from the concrete reality of its everyday existence than the salariat' (p. 110). The German reads: 'der konkreten Wirklichkeit Alltags entfremdeter' (p. 220).

72. Walter Benjamin, 'Moscow', in *One Way Street*, p. 189.

73. See for example the memoirs of Rosa Leviné-Meyer, *Inside German Communism: Memoirs of Party Life in the Weimar Republic*, edited and introduced by David Zane Mairowitz (London: Pluto Press, 1977).

74. Boris Arvatov, *Kunst und Produktion* (Karl Hanser Verlag, 1972).

75. Arvatov published *Iskusstvo i klassy* (*Art and Classes*) in 1923, *Iskusstvo i proizvodstvo* (*Art and Production*) in 1926, *Sociologiceskaja poetika* (*Sociological Poetry*) in 1928, and *Ob agit i proziskusstva* (*Productivist Art and Agitation*) in 1930.

76. Arvatov, *Kunst und Produktion*, p. 19.

77. Ibid., p. 9.

78. Ibid., p. 10.

79. Ibid., p. 23.

80. Ibid., p. 27.

81. Ibid., p. 33.

82. Ibid., p. 35.

83. Ibid., p. 36.

84. Ibid., p. 64.

85. Leon Trotsky, 'The Cultural Role of the Worker Correspondent', in *Problems*, p. 164.

86. In *My Life* (New York: Pathfinder, 1970) Trotsky described her as having the 'courage of a warrior'.

87. Larissa Reissner, *Hamburg at the Barricades, and other writings on Weimar Germany*, translated and edited by Richard Chappell (London: Pluto Press, 1977). First published in 1925 by Neue Deutsche as *Hamburg auf den Barrikaden: Erlebtes und Erhörtes aus dem Hamburger Aufstand* 1923, this is a brilliantly vivid, and the most widely read account of the Hamburg uprising. Reissner entered Germany from the Soviet Union in 1923 and lived with workers during the abortive rising in Hamburg in 1923. As a communist journalist she went down the mines (in the Ruhr) and participated in factory meetings of factory boards, shop committees and trade unions. She died in 1926.

88. Reissner, *Hamburg at the Barricades*, p. 62.

89. As Benjamin says in 'A Small History of Photography', 'Now, to bring things *closer* to us, or rather to the masses, is just as passionate an inclination in our days as the overcoming of whatever is unique in every situation by means of its reproduction. Everyday the need to possess the object in close-up in the form of a picture, or rather a copy, becomes more imperative.' *One Way Street*, p. 250.

90. As is well known it is Jünger whom Benjamin is most probably thinking of at the end of 'The Art Work in the Age of Mechanical Reproduction', when he discusses Fascism and aesthetics. *Illuminations*, p. 235.

91. In *Der gefährliche Augenblick: Eine Sammlung von Bildern und Berichten*, 200 Seiten mit über 100 Abbildungen, herausgegeben von Ferdinand Bucholtz, Einleitung von Ernst Jünger (Berlin: Junder & Dünnhaupt Verlag, 1931); *Das Antlitz des Weltkrieges: Fronterlebnisse deutscher Soldaten*, mit etwa 200 Photographischen, Aufnahmen auf Tafeln, Kartenanhang sowie einer chronologischen Kriegsgeschichte in Tabelle, herausgegeben von Ernst Jünger (Berlin: Neufeld & Henias Verlag, 1930); *Die Veränderte Welt: Eine Bilderfibel unserer Zeit*, herausgegeben von Edmund Schultz, Einleitung von Ernst Jünger (Breslau: Whil. Gottl. Korn Verlag, 1933).

92. Lukács, *History and Class Consciousness*, p. 9.

2 The Everyday as Trace and Remainder

1. Walter Benjamin, *The Arcades Project*, translated by Howard Eiland and Kevin McLaughlin (Cambridge, Massachusetts: Harvard University Press, 1999).

2. Walter Benjamin, 'The Work of Art in the Age of Mechanical Reproduction', in *Illuminations* (London: Fontana, 1973), p. 237.

3. See for example, *On The Interpretation of Dreams* (Harmondsworth: Pelican, 1976 [1900]).

4. For a discussion of this issue, see Peter Osborne, 'Small-scale Victories, Large-scale Defeats: Walter Benjamin's Politics of Time', in Andrew Benjamin and Peter Osborne (eds), *Walter Benjamin's Philosophy: Destruction and Experience* (London: Routledge, 1994).

5. F. W. J. Schelling, *Philosophical Inquiries into the Nature of Human Freedom* (La Salle, Illinois: Open Court, 1986 [1809]), p. 34.

6. Ibid.

7. Henri Lefebvre, 'La Mystification: Notes pour une critique de la vie quotidienne', *Avant-Poste*, No. 2 (August 1933).

8. Henri Lefebvre, *The Critique of Everyday Life, Vol. 1* (London and New York: Verso,1991).

9. Henri Lefebvre, 'Towards a Leftist Cultural Politics: Remarks Occasioned by the Centenary of Marx's Death', in *Marxism and the Interpretation of Culture*, edited and with an introduction by Cary Nelson and Lawrence Grossberg (Chicago: University of Illinois Press, 1988), p. 86.

10. Lefebvre, 'Towards a Leftist Cultural Politics', p. 83. In this respect see also *Everyday Life in the Modern World*, translated by Sacha Rabinovitch and with a new introduction by Philip Wander (London: Athlone Press, 2000 [1968]).

11. Lefebvre, *The Critique of Everyday Life, Vol. II: Foundations for a Sociology of the Everyday*, p. 19.

12. See, in particular, André Breton's *Nadja* (Paris: Gallimard, 1964).

13. For an analysis of postwar French modernization and the 'everyday', see Kristin Ross, *Fast Cars, Clean Bodies: Decolonization and The Reordering of French Culture* (Cambridge, Massachusetts and London: MIT Press, 1995).

14. Roland Barthes, *Mythologies* (Paris: Editions du Seuil, 1957).

15. Ibid., p. 9.

16. Jean-Paul Sartre, *Being and Nothingness* (London, Methuen, 1969 [1943]), p. 506.

17. See, for example, Erich Weil, *Hegel et l'Etat: Cinq conférences suivres de 'Marx et le philosophie du droit'* (Paris: Librairie Philosophique, J. Vrin, 1950). Published in English as *Hegel and the State*, translated by Mark A. Cohen (Baltimore: Johns Hopkins University Press, 1998).

18. G. W. F. Hegel, *The Phenomenology of Spirit*, translated by A. V. Miller with a foreword by J. N. Finlay (Oxford: Oxford University Press 1977 [1807]).

19. Simone de Beauvoir, *The Second Sex* (London: New English Library, 1969 [1949]), p. 331.

20. Ibid., p. 464.

21. Maurice Blanchot, *L'Entretien infini* (Paris: Gallimard, 1959). The section on Lefebvre and the everyday was translated and published as 'Everyday Speech', *Yale French Studies*, No. 73 (1987).

22. Blanchot, 'Everyday Speech', p. 13.

23. Ibid., p. 13.

24. Ibid., p. 15.

25. Ibid., p. 17.

26. *L'Internationale Situationniste: 1958–69* (Amsterdam: Van Gennep, 1970).

27. The Situationists were also outraged by Lefebvre's foolish characterization of the group in *Introduction a la modernité* (1962) as a youth organization.

28. Guy Debord, *La Société du Spectacle* (Paris: Buchet-Chastel, 1967). English translation, *The Society of the Spectacle* (Detroit: Black and Red, 1977).

29. 'The Transformation of Everyday Life', from *IS*, No. 6 (1961), reprinted in Christopher Gray (ed.), *Leaving the Twentieth Century: The Incomplete Work of the Situationist International* (London: Free Fall Publications, 1974).

30. Ibid., p. 38.
31. Attila Kontanyi and Raoul Vaneigem, 'Unitary Urbanism', *IS*, No. 6 (1961), in Gray, *Leaving the Twentieth Century*, p. 30.
32. Lefebvre, *The Critique of Everyday Life*, Vol. I.
33. Guy Debord, 'Rapport dur la construction des situations', in *L'Internationalionale Situationniste: 1958–69*.
34. Raoul Vaneigem, *The Revolution of Everyday Life* (Edinburgh: Left Bank Books and Rebel Press, 1983).
35. The theory of state capitalism argues that the value-form (competition between enterprises; exploitation at the point of production; technological direction and constraint of labour power) operated in the old Soviet Union, even though the economy was not subject to an internal market.
36. Vaneigem, *Revolution*, p. 168.
37. Schelling, *Philosophical Inquiries*, p. 80.
38. Vaneigem, *Revolution*, p. 151.
39. Ibid., p. 45.
40. Ibid., p. 150.
41. Ibid., p. 149.
42. Ibid., p. 126.
43. It is hard to reconstruct the political relations between Lefebvre and the Situationists with any accuracy. Lefebvre certainly influenced the formation of the SI, giving some philosophical shape to their cultural categories. But the SI, in turn, certainly pulled Lefebvre further to the left; that is, many of his prewar cultural affiliations and reflexes were grounded in a humanist–realist critique of the avant-garde.
44. Vaneigem, *Revolution*, p. 177.
45. Michel de Certeau, *L'Invention du quotidien, Vol. 1: Arts de Faire* (Paris: Gallimard, 1974). *The Practice of Everyday Life*, translated by Steven Randall (University of California Press, 1984).
46. Michel de Certeau, *La Culture au pluriel* (Paris: Union Générale d'Editions, 1974. *Culture in the Plural*, introduced by Luce Giard and translated by Tom Conley (Minneapolis: University of Minnesota Press, 1997).
47. De Certeau, *Practice*, p. xix.
48. Ibid., p. 26.
49. Ibid., p. xiv.
50. Ibid., p. 28.
51. Ibid., p. 18.
52. Ibid., p. xvii.
53. Ibid., p. 98.
54. Ibid., p. 110.
55. Ibid., p. 40.
56. Félix Guattari, 'Towards a Micro-Politics of Desire' [1975], in *Le Révolution moléculaire* (Paris, Editions Recherches, 1977).

English translation, *Molecular Revolution: Psychiatry and Politics* (Harmondsworth: Penguin, 1984), p. 87.

57. Guattari, *Molecular Revolution*, p. 84.
58. Ibid., pp. 86–7.
59. De Certeau, *Practice*, p. 4.
60. Ibid., p. 5.
61. See, in particular, Jacques Derrida, *La Dissémination* (Paris: Editions du Seuil, 1972); English translation, *Disseminations*, translated by Barbara Johnson (London: Athlone Press, 1981).
62. Lefebvre, *Everyday Life in the Modern World*, p. 156.
63. See Claude Lévi-Strauss, *Tristes Tropiques*, translated by John Russell (London: Hutchinson, 1961).
64. See, for instance, Detlev J. K. Peukert, *Inside Nazi Germany: Conformity, Opposition and Racism in Everyday Life* (Harmondsworth: Pelican, 1980).
65. In Britain this historiography of resistance 'from below' was developed largely by E. P. Thompson from the 1960s in his work on popular custom. In Thompson the everyday is analysed as the actual site of the cultural contestability of capitalism, rescuing the everyday practices and historical agency of the labouring poor from condescension. In his later work on the eighteenth century, for example, Thompson treats widespread acts of 'pilfering' as the outcome of a disputed claim on the part of the poor about the collection of 'waste' from production as a customary right. As such he treats the resistance of the poor to the emerging new capitalist economy as a form of counter-rationality. It has to be said, though, that Thompson made no attempt to link his work intellectually with the 'critique of everyday life' – to the work's theoretical detriment. See *Customs in Common* (London: Merlin, 1991).
66. This position had some influence on a post-Thompson history 'from below' in Britain in the 1980s. For example, Patrick Wright's *On Living in an Old Country: The National Past in Contemporary Britain* (London and New York: Verso, 1985) argues that historical consciousness of the everyday is constantly detaching itself from the dominant national tradition, just as the dominant national tradition is continually reassessing its ideological content under pressure 'from below'.

3 Lefebvre's Dialectical Irony: Marx and the Everyday

1. *Critique de la vie quotidienne II: Fondements d'une sociologie de la quotidienneté* (Paris: L'Arche Editeur, 1961), translated as *The Critique of Everyday Life, Vol. II: Foundations for a Sociology of the Everyday*; *Introduction a la modernité* (Paris: Les Editions de Minuit, 1962), translated by John Moore as *Introduction to*

Modernity: Twelve Preludes (London and New York: Verso, 1995); *De la vie quotidienne et le monde moderne* (Paris: 1967), translated by Sacha Rabinovitch and with a new introduction by Philip Wander as *Everyday Life in the Modern World* (London: Athlone, 2000); *Sociologie de Marx* (Paris: Presses Universitaires de France, 1966), translated as *The Sociology of Marx* (Harmondsworth: Allen Lane, Penguin Press, 1968).

2. Lefebvre, *The Critique of Everyday Life*, Vol. II, p. 35.
3. Ibid., p. 37.
4. Ibid., p. 23.
5. Ibid., p. 28.
6. Ibid., p. 160.
7. Ibid., p. 85.
8. See G. W. F. Hegel, *The Science of Logic*, translated by William Wallace, with a foreword by J. N. Findlay (Oxford: Oxford University Press, 1975).
9. Lefebvre, *Introduction to Modernity*, p. 11.
10. Ibid., p. 15.
11. Ibid., p. 25.
12. Ibid., p. 37.
13. Ibid., p. 203.
14. Georg Lukács, *A Defence of* History of Class Consciousness: *Tailism and the Dialectic*, translated by Esther Leslie and with an introduction by John Rees and a postface by Slavoj Žižek (London and New York: Verso, 2000).
15. Lefebvre, *Everyday Life in the Modern World*, p. 145.
16. Ibid., pp. 188–9.
17. Ibid., p. 172.
18. Ibid., pp. 30–1.
19. Ibid, p. 204.
20. Ibid., p. 203.
21. Lefebvre, *The Critique of Everyday Life*, Vol. II, p. 348.
22. Ibid, p. 219.
23. Ibid., p. 222.
24. Lefebvre, *Introduction to Modernity*, p. 345.
25. Karl Marx, 'Economic and Philosophic Manuscripts of 1844', in Karl Marx and Frederick Engels, *Collected Works*, Vol. 3 (London: Lawrence & Wishart, 1975).
26. Ibid., p. 343.
27. Lefebvre, *The Critique of Everyday Life*, Vol. II, p. 185.
28. See Lukács, *Tailism and the Dialectic*.
29. Georg Lukács, quoted by David Frisby in his introduction to Georg Simmel, *The Philosophy of Money*, translated by Tom Bottomore and David Frisby (London: Routledge & Kegan Paul, 1978), p. 20.

30. See Georg Lukács, 'Technology and Social Relations', *New Left Review*, No. 39 (September/October 1966).

31. For an extended discussion of this theme in Benjamin, see Esther Leslie, *Walter Benjamin: Overpowering Conformism* (London: Pluto Press, 2000).

32. However, this is not to say that Lefebvre's writing, in contrast to other philosophers of the period, did not have an enormous influence on actual practice. *De la vie quotidienne dans le monde moderne*, for instance, found a large readership on its publication in 1968 (Paris: Gallimard), particularly after May '68: for in its summary form it provides a polemical defence of the utopian content of the critique of the everyday as part of an attack on postwar French modernization. In this, in its emphasis on the renewed agency of the working class, on a nascent women's liberation, the power of the electronic image and the 'crisis' of the neo-avant-garde, it provided one of the theoretical templates for the student movement and what was to become the New Left in the 1970s in the United States. See, for example, Bruce Brown's excellent *Marx, Freud and the Critique of Everyday Life: Toward a Permanent Cultural Revolution* (London and New York: Monthly Review Press, 1973). Brown's book was the first in English to give systematic attention to the postwar debate on the everyday, providing one of the first entry points into the writings of Lefebvre, Vaneigem and Debord – whose work had yet to be assimilated critically by the left. Also, along with *Sociologie dans Marx, De la vie quotidienne dans le monde moderne* was translated into English during this period. In this respect the slogans of the Situationist International may have come to define the iconoclastic character of May 1968, but it was Lefebvre's writing that did much to shape the cultural and political landscape that brought the influence of the Situationists to critical prominence.

Epilogue

1. Another good example of the increasing ecumenical content of the concept in the 1970s is Agnes Heller's *Everyday Life* (London: Routledge & Kegan Paul, 1984). Written in 1967–68, and first published in Hungarian in 1970, *Everyday Life* is heavily indebted to the Lukácsian cultural origins of the debate on the everyday, but is also strongly critical of his messianism. Heller transforms the critique of the everyday into a kind of communal actionism: the everyday becomes the collective space of the free, rational–reflective agency of individuals. Advocating the importance of localized, cultural change above macro-change, she argues 'how everyday life can be changed in a humanistic, democratic socialist direction' (p. x).

Bibliography

Anderson, Perry, *Considerations on Western Marxism* (London and New York: New Left Books, 1976).

Aronowitz, Stanley, *Roll Over Beethoven: The Return of Cultural Studies* (Hanover, New England: Wesleyan University Press, 1993).

Arvatov, Boris, *Kunst und Produktion* (Munich: Karl Hanser Verlag, 1972 [1926]).

Barthes, Roland, *Mythologies* (Paris: Éditions du Seuil, 1957).

Benjamin, Andrew, and Osborne, Peter (eds), *Walter Benjamin's Philosophy: Destruction and Experience* (London and New York: Routledge, 1994).

Benjamin, Walter, *Illuminations* (London: Fontana, 1973).

Benjamin, Walter, *Aufsätze, Essays, Vorträge: Gesammelte Schriften Band 2.3* (Frankfurt am Main: Suhrkamp, 1977).

Benjamin, Walter, *One Way Street and Other Writings*, translated by Edmund Jephcott and Kingsley Shorter (London: New Left Books, 1979).

Benjamin, Walter, *Nachträge: Gesammelte Schirften, Band 2.2* (Frankfurt am Main: Suhrkamp, 1989).

Benjamin, Walter, *Kritiken under Rezensionen: Gesemmalte Schriften Band 3* (Frankfurt am Main: Suhrkamp, 1991).

Benjamin, Walter, *The Arcades Project*, translated by Howard Eiland and Kevin McLaughlin (Cambridge, Massachusetts: Harvard University Press, 1999).

Blanchot, Maurice, *L'Entretien infini* (Paris: Gallimard, 1959).

Blanchot, Maurice, 'Everyday Speech', in *Yale French Studies*, No. 73 (1987).

Bowlt, John E., 'Manipulating Metaphors: El Lissitzky and the Crafted Hand', in Nancy Perloff and Brian Reed (eds), *Situating El Lissitzky: Vitebsk, Berlin, Moscow* (Los Angeles: Getty Research Institute, 2003).

Breton, André, *Nadja* (Paris: Gallimard, 1964).

Brown, Bruce, *Marx, Freud and the Critique of Everyday Life: Toward a Permanent Cultural Revolution* (London and New York: Monthly Review Press, 1973).

Chaney, David, *Cultural Change and Everyday Life* (London: Palgrave, 2002).

Ciliga, Ante, *The Russian Enigma*, part one translated by Fernand G. Fernier and Anne Cliff, part two translated by Margaret and Hugo Dewar (London: Ink Links, 1979 [1938]).

De Beauvoir, Simone, *The Second Sex,* translated and edited by H.M. Parshley (London: New English Library, 1969 [1949]).

Debord, Guy, *La Sociétié du Spectacle* (Paris: Buchet-Chastel, 1967).

Debord, Guy, *The Society of the Spectacle* (Detroit: Black and Red, 1977).

De Certeau, Michel, *La Culture au pluriel* (Paris: Union Générale d'Editions, 1974).

De Certeau, Michel, *L'Invention du quotidien, Vol. 1, Arts de Faire* (Paris: Gallimard, 1974).

De Certeau, Michel, *The Practice of Everyday Life*, translated by Steven F. Rendall (Berkeley: University of California Press, 1984).

De Certeau, Michel, *Culture in the Plural*, introduced by Luce Giard and translated by Tom Conley (Minneapolis: University of Minnesota Press, 1997).

Derrida, Jacques, *La Dissémination* (Paris: Editions du Seuil, 1972).

Derrida, Jacques, *Disseminations*, translated by Barbara Johnson (London: Athlone Press, 1981).

Engels, Frederick, *Ludwig Feuerbach and the End of Classical Philosophy* (Peking: Foreign Language Press, 1976 [1888]).

Freud, Sigmund, *The Interpretation of Dreams* (Harmondsworth: Penguin, 1900).

Freud, Sigmund, *The Psychopathology of Everyday Life* (London and Glasgow: Collins, 1958 [1901]).

Freud, Sigmund, *The Standard Edition of the Complete Psychological Works*, 24 vols, Vol. 11 (London: Hogarth Press and the Institute of Psychoanalysis, 1953–74).

Fülöp-Miller, René, *The Mind and Face of Bolshevism: An Examination of Cultural Life in Soviet Russia*, translated by F.S. Flint and D.F. Tait (London and New York: G.P. Putnam's Sons, 1927).

Gramsci, Antonio, *Selections from the Prison Notebooks*, edited and translated by Quintin Hoare and Geoffrey Nowell Smith (London: Lawrence and Wishart, 1971).

Gray, Christopher (ed.), *Leaving the Twentieth Century: The Incomplete Work of the Situationist International* (London: Free Fall Publications, 1974).

Guattari, Félix, 'Towards a Micro-Politics of Desire', in *Molecular Revolution: Psychiatry and Politics* (Harmondsworth: Penguin, 1984 [1975]).

Hegel, G.W.F., *The Science of Logic*, translated by William Wallace, with foreword by J.N. Findlay (Oxford: Oxford University Press, 1975).

Hegel, G.W.F., *The Phenomenology of Spirit*, translated by A.V. Miller, with foreword by J.N. Findlay (Oxford: Oxford University Press, 1977 [1807]).

Heller, Agnes, *Everyday Life* (London: Routledge & Kegan Paul, 1984 [1970]).

Heidegger, Martin, *Being and Time* (Oxford: Basil Blackwell, 1962).

Heidegger, Martin, *The Question Concerning Technology and Other Essays*, translated and with an introduction by William Lovitt (London and New York: Harper & Row, 1977).

Highmore, Ben, *Everyday Life and Cultural Theory: An Introduction* (London and New York: Routledge, 2002).

Jünger, Ernst (ed.), *Das Antlitz des Weltkrieges: Fronterlebnisse deutscher Soldaten* (Berlin: Neufeld & Henias Verlag, 1930).

Jünger, Ernst, *In Der gefährliche Augenblick: Eine sammlung von Bildern und Berichten*, herausgegeben von Ferdinand Bucholtz, Einleitung von Ernst Jünger (Berlin: Junder & Dünnhaupt Verlag, 1931).

Jünger, Ernst, *Die Veränderte Welt: Eine Bilderfibel unserer Zeit*, herausgegeben von Edmund Schultz, Einleitung von Ernst Jünger (Beslau: Whil. Gottl. Korn Verlag, 1933).

Kollantai, Alexandra, *Red Love* (New York: Seven Arts Publishing Co., 1927 [1923]).

Kollontai, Alexandra, *The Autobiography of a Sexually Emancipated Communist Woman*, translated by Salvator Attensio (New York: Herder & Herder, 1971).

Kollantai, Alexandra, 'Marriage and Everyday Life', in *Alexandra Kollantai: Selected Writings*, translated and with commentaries by Alix Holt (London: Allison & Busby, 1977).

Kollantai, Alexandra, *Love of Worker Bees*, with an introduction by Cathy Porter and an afterword by Sheila Rowbotham (London: Virago, 1977).

Korsch, Karl, *Marxism and Philosophy* (London: New Left Books, 1970 [1923]).

Kracauer, Siegried, *The Salaried Masses: Duty and Distraction in Weimar Germany*, translated by Quintin Hoare and introduced by Inka Mülder-Bach (London and New York: Verso, 1998 [1930]).

Kraniauskas, John, 'Globalization is Ordinary', *Radical Philosophy*, No. 90 (July/August 1998).

Lefebvre, Henri, 'La Mystification: Notes pour une critique de la vie quotidienne', *Avant-Poste*, No. 2 (August 1933).

Lefebvre, Henri, *Critique de la vie quotidienne II: Fondements d'une sociologie de la quotidienneté* (Paris: L'Arche Editeur, 1961).

Lefebvre, Henri, *Introduction a la modernité* (Paris: Les Editions de Minuit, 1962).

Lefebvre, Henri, *Sociologie de* Marx (Paris: Presse Universitaires de France, 1966).

Lefebvre, Henri, *Dialectical Materialism* (London: Jonathan Cape, 1968 [1940]).

Lefebvre, Henri, *The Sociology of Marx* (Harmondsworth: Allen Lane, Penguin Press, 1968).

Lefebvre, Henri, *Critique de la vie quotidienne III. De la modernité au modernisme (Pour une metaphilosophie de quotidien)* (Paris: L'Arche Editeur, 1981).

Lefebvre, Henri, 'Towards a Leftist Cultural Politics: Remarks Occasioned by the Centenary of Marx's Death', in *Marxism and the Interpretation of Culture*, edited and with an introduction by Cary Nelson and Lawrence Grossberg (Urbana: University of Illinois Press, 1988).

Lefebvre, Henri, *Critique of Everyday Life, Vol. 1* (London and New York: Verso, 1991 [1947]).

Lefebvre, Henri, *Introduction to Modernity: Twelve Preludes*, translated by John Moore (London and New York: Verso, 1995 [1962]).

Lefebvre, Henri, *Everyday Life in the Modern World*, translated by Sacha Rabinovitch, with a new introduction by Philip Wander (London: Athlone Press, 2000 [1968]).

Lefebvre, Henri, *The Critique of Everyday Life, Vol. II: Foundations for a Sociology of the Everyday,* translated by John Moore, with a preface by Michel Trebitsch (London and New York: Verso, 2002 [1961]).

Lenin, V.I., 'Immediate Tasks of the Soviet Government', in *Collected Works, Vol. 27* (Moscow: Progress Publishers, 1972).

Leslie, Esther, *Walter Benjamin: Overpowering Conformism* (London: Pluto Press, 2000).

Leviné-Meyer, Rosa, *Inside German Communism: Memoirs of Party Life in the Weimar Republic*, edited and introduced by David Zane Mairowitz (London: Pluto Press, 1977).

Lévi-Strauss, Claude, *Tristes Tropiques*, translated by John Russell (London: Hutchinson, 1961).

Lukács, Georg, 'Technology and Social Relations', *New Left Review*, No.39 (September/October 1966).

Lukács, Georg, *Lenin: A Study on the Unity of His Thought* (London: New Left Books, 1970 [1924]).

Lukács, Georg, *Theory of the Novel* (London: Merlin Press, 1971).

Lukács, Georg, *History and Class Consciousness: Studies in Marxist Dialectics* (London: Merlin Press, 1971 [1923]).

Lukács, Georg, *Conversations with Lukács,* edited by Theo Pinkus (London: Merlin Press, 1974).

Lukács, Georg, *A Defence of* History of Class Consciousness: *Tailism and the Dialectic'*, translated by Esther Leslie, with an introduction by John Rees and a postface by Slavoj Žižek (London and New York: Verso, 2000).

MacKay, Hugh (ed.), *Consumption and Everyday Life* (London: Sage Publications, in association with the Open University, 1997).

Margolin, Victor, *The Struggle For Utopia: Rodchenko, Lissitzky, Moholy-nagy 1917–1946* (Chicago: University of Chicago Press, 1997).

Márkus, György, 'Life and the Soul: the Young Lukács and the Problem of Culture', in Agnes Heller (ed.) *Lukács Revalued* (Oxford: Basil Blackwell, 1983).

Marx, Karl, *A Contribution to the Critique of Political Economy*, translated by N.I. Stone (Chicago: Charles H. Kerr Publishing, 1904).

Marx, Karl, *Capital, Vol. 1* (London: Lawrence & Wishart, 1970).

Marx, Karl, *Grundrisse* (Harmondsworth: Penguin, 1973).

Marx, Karl, 'Economic and Philosophic Manuscripts of 1844', in Karl Marx and Frederick Engels, *Collected Works, Vol. 3* (London: Lawrence & Wishart, 1975).

Massumi, Brian (ed.), *The Politics of Everyday Fear* (Minneapolis: University of Minnesota Press, 1993).

Metz, Johann Baptist, 'Prophetic Authority', in Jürgen Moltmann, Herbert W. Richardson, Johann Baptist Metz, Willi Oelmüller and M. Darrol Bryant, *Religion and Political Society* (London and New York: Harper & Row, 1974).

Perkins, Stephen, *Marxism and the Proletariat: A Lukácsian Perspective* (London and Boulder, Colorado: Pluto Press, 1993).

Peukert, Detlev J.K., *Inside Nazi Germany: Conformity, Opposition and Racism in Everyday Life* (Harmondsworth: Pelican, 1980).

Reissner, Larissa, *Hamburg auf den Barrikaden: Erlebtes und Erhörtes aus dem Hamburger Aufstand 1923* (Hamburg: Neue Deutsche, 1925).

Reissner, Larissa, *Hamburg at the Barricades, and other writings on Weimar Germany*, translated and edited by Richard Chappell (London: Pluto Press, 1977).

Remington, Thomas F., *Building Socialism in Bolshevik Russia: Ideology and Industrial Organization 1917–1921* (Pittsburgh and London: University of Pittsburgh Press, 1984).

Roberts, John, *The Art of Interruption: Realism, Photography and the Everyday* (Manchester: Manchester University Press, 1998).

Ross, Kristin, *Fast Cars, Clean Bodies: Decolonization and The Reordering of French Culture* (Cambridge, Massachusetts, and London: MIT Press, 1995).

Ross, Kristin, 'Streetwise: the French Invention of Everyday Life', *Parallax*, No. 2 (1996).

Ross Kristin, 'French Quotidian', in Lynn Gumpert (ed.), *The Art of the Everyday: The Quotidian in Postwar French Culture* (New York: New York University Press, 1997).

Ross Kristin, *May '68 and Its Afterlives* (Chicago and London: Chicago University Press, 2002).

Sartre, Jean-Paul, *Being and Nothingness* (London: Methuen, 1969 [1943]).

Schwartz, Frederic J., *The Werkbund: Design Theory and Mass Culture before the First World War* (New Haven: Yale University Press, 1996).

Schelling, F.W.J., *Philosophical Inquiries Into the Nature of Human Freedom* (La Salle, Illinois: Open Court, 1986 [1809]).

Serge, Victor, *Year One of the Russian Revolution*, translated and edited by Peter Sedgwick with a new preface by Paul Foot (London and New York: Bookmarks/Pluto Press/Writers and Readers, 1992 [1930]).

Simmel, Georg, *The Philosophy of Money*, translated by Tom Bottomore and David Frisby (London and New York: Routledge & Kegan Paul, 1978 [1907]).

Situationist International, *L'Internationalionale Situationniste: 1958–69* (Amsterdam: Van Gennep, 1970).

Tafuri, Manfredo, *Architecture and Utopia: Design and Capitalist Development*, translated by Barbara Luiga La Penta (Cambridge, Massachusetts, and London: MIT Press, 1976).

Thompson, E.P., *Customs in Common* (London: Merlin Press, 1991).

Trotsky, Leon, *Problems of Everyday Life, and Other Writings on Culture and Science* (New York: Pathfinder Press, 1973 [1923]).

Trotsky, Leon, *History of the Russian Revolution* (New York: Pathfinder Press, 1980).

Vaneigem, Raoul, *The Revolution of Everyday Life* (Edinburgh: Left Bank Distribution and Rebel Press, 1983 [1967]).

Vazquez, Adolfo Sánchez, *The Philosophy of Praxis*, translated by Mike Gonzalez (London and New Jersey: Merlin Press, 1977 [1966]).

Volishinov, V.N., *Freudianism: A Marxist Critique*, translated by I.R.Titunik and edited in collaboration with Neal H. Bruss (New York: Academic Press, 1976).

Weil, Erich, *Hegel and the State*, translated by Mark A. Cohen (Baltimore: Johns Hopkins University Press, 1998 [1950]).

Wright Patrick, *On Living in an Old Country: The National Past in Contemporary Britain* (London and New York: Verso, 1985).

Zalambani, Maria, 'Boris Arvatov, Théoricien Du Productivisme', *Cahiers du monde russe*, 40/3 (July/September, 1999).

Index